ANYTHING But Normal

The Unusual Life of Uno the Miracle Dog

Mark Reed

author of "The True You," "Lighten Up" and "Let's Get Metaphysical"

Anything But Normal:

The Unusual Life of Uno the Miracle Dog

- 2 -

Copyright ©2020 Mark Reed

ISBN: 9798648684416
Imprint: Independently published

That night, as Uno lay in bed with Deb, he had an astonishing, awe-inspiring dream. It was one of those epic dreams, an all-night adventure. He dreamed that spirits from another world came to him. They silently hovered over him, and then he felt a jolt in his body like one of the spirits thumped his head. He woke up abruptly. The experience was surreal. He fell asleep again immediately and dreamed he was a beggar in ancient Mesopotamia, then a priest in Egypt, then a disciple of the philosopher Plotinus, a farmer in China, and a warrior in Mongolia. It was a very realistic dream with sights, sounds, and smells, and seemed to last forever. When Uno awoke the next morning, something was different.

To Russ, on his Pogo Stick. My editor, book and cover designer.
(russphillips@csourcedesign.com)

To Deb Welker Miller and Ben Miller, for lending photos of
Baxter (our model for the Miracle Dog), and Django.

To Jane, for your loving guidance as I healed this past year.
Thank you for helping me remember my truth.

To Reverend Karen, for believing in me.

To Dora: My love.

Table of Contents

Foreword

"The way a person does one thing is the way they do everything." This quote comes to mind when I think of Mark Reed. He's been a valued spiritual practitioner at the West Valley Center for Spiritual Living in Peoria, Arizona for 11 years. I've known him for five years now and have personally witnessed his personal growth. He is a light-hearted, genuine man committed to his own and others' spiritual growth. Put simply, Mark loves people and enjoys helping them traverse their spiritual path.

When I first met Mark, I experienced a loving welcome from him and could tell he had a genuine interest in me. He connects with people on a deeper level as he gets to know them and enjoys sharing their personal journey. Mark is very open and honest about his life experiences, challenges, and successes, which creates a safe place for people to open up and share their personal story. His ability to connect with people and accept them, right where they are, opens the door for conversations about the most important things in life. He is a teacher at heart, and enjoys helping people see their spiritual truth, regardless of perceived conditions. His primary intention is to create a loving bond to love, honor, and support people.

We are all on a spiritual journey of discovery of sorts to understand who we are and why we're here. It's all about the journey. I truly believe that every person we meet and every experience we have serves one purpose—to remind us of our truth. Each of us is a beautiful, individualized expression of God. It takes us time to realize this truth, and then it takes practice to live from that realization. When we remember our true identity and accept it, our spirituality deepens, and life become easier. Easier doesn't mean we're free from challenges, obstacles, and errors in thinking—it means we know we're never alone, that nothing is too big for God, and that our consciousness is evolving to a higher expression of life. We teach spiritual principles and practices so that we can live the life we want to experience.

Mark is a licensed Religious Science practitioner who has committed his life to spiritual growth. As a practitioner, he has dedicated himself to serving our community. Life gives us plenty of opportunities to move through our mental obstacles to a higher thought plane. This book is a reflection of the spiritual work Mark has experienced while exploring his expanding faith.

Mark stayed true to himself while writing this book. The main character, Uno, is a beautiful and heart-centered dog grounded in spiritual principle. Like Mark, he enjoys helping people along their path. Each chapter reflects a life that's jam packed with joy and love as expressed through the eyes of a dog. Uno is a perfect representation of unconditional love. Dogs really are the best teachers.

As the book progresses, Mark opens up your heart and creates a safe place. Then he explores different life experiences and conditions that might be a challenge in your life. At the end of each chapter, he writes a powerful affirmative prayer that reminds you of your truth and provides several affirmations that you can use to heal your mind. He even adds rhyming affirmations to remind you to lighten up and be gentle with yourself as you move through similar conditions. He wraps up each chapter with Uno's reflections on the spiritual truth of the situation.

This book touched me on many different levels. I found myself loving Uno and enjoying his journey. Each chapter allowed me to reflect on personal experiences and reminded me of my truth. The rhyming affirmations made me smile and chuckle. It's a great read for all ages and a book everyone should add to his or her spiritual toolbox. Mark has not only provided us with spiritual principles and affirmations that can help us through life, he gave us a loving and furry messenger of Universal Truth. Good job, my friend.

Reverend Clyde Goins, West Valley Center for Spiritual Living
March 2020

Preface

"That night, as Uno lay in bed with Deb, he had an astonishing, awe-inspiring dream. It was one of those epic dreams, an all-night adventure."

Uno's dream is an echo of a similar experience I had in the fall of 2019. I had an astonishing, awe-inspiring, epic dream. It was about a dog, but not your everyday, run-of-the-mill type dog. This unique canine could think like a human. More than that, he was capable of reading people's thoughts and communicating telepathically with the subconscious minds of his human companions.

Yeah, it was a wild dream—very realistic.

In my dream, the dog snuggled up to people who were experiencing mental and emotional distress and "knew their truth for them." I've been a CSL (Centers for Spiritual Living) spiritual practitioner for 11 years now. That's what we do. Well, not the snuggling up part, but we know people's truth for them when they ask for our assistance.

A cynic might ask, "Whose truth are we talking about here? Your truth? My truth? Who's to say what truth is, anyway?" These questions go to the heart of New Thought philosophy. If you're unfamiliar with the spiritual faith traditions we call New Thought, I suggest you Google the term. I found a New Thought faith that works for me 14 years ago. This spiritual philosophy has been the yellow brick road that I've been singing and dancing down ever since. It has taken me to incredible spiritual heights.

Likewise, Uno is on a spiritual journey. Like many of us, he questions his existence. "Why am I here? What is my life purpose? When am I getting more bacon strips?"

Writing a piece of fiction was the furthest thing from my mind, but the dream I experienced led me to believe this story was Spirit inspired. Who knows, maybe there were spiritual beings from the afterlife, hovering over me as I was lying in bed, planting these images and ideas into my head. That's a cool visual, isn't it? Or maybe I'm just a bit self-absorbed and "way out there."

My dog dream was a kick in the butt. I had to write this story. I knew the practitioner and prayer aspect would be easy for me to write. I do that all the time. My fingers were flying on the keyboard at the end of each chapter when Uno affirmatively prays for his new friend. Writing 500 plus affirmations was an enjoyable spiritual experience as well; and creating the rhyming affirmations was just plain fun. But the story itself, the characters, the prose—that was a challenge.

They say that a writer should write about what's most familiar to him or her. I don't know who "they" are, but that's what I decided to do. The story takes place in my hometown of Macomb, Illinois. From age 22 onward, my wife Dora and I lived in Texas, Southern California, Northern California, England, Iceland, Saudi Arabia, and now Phoenix, Arizona. In the summer of '97, I did an internship at Columbia University and lived on the upper West side of Manhattan for ten weeks. That was fun! But none of these places compare with my hometown. I have several painful and scary memories of Macomb, but the majority are heartwarming, innocent, fun, and inspiring. I grew up there from age 11 to 21—my formative years.

The story is set in 1976, the year I graduated from Macomb High School. 1975 and 1976 were two of the most fun and social years of my life. It was a simpler time. There were only three channels on TV. We weren't confused about how to configure software, design a web page, or stream music and videos. We didn't have email, we had post-it notes, and we weren't addicted to our phones. In fact, our phones weren't even mini-computers—they were just phones. They had these irritating cords on them that became a tangled mess if you walked to the other side of the room while on the phone. Okay, I'm officially an old fart. If you're under age 40, don't laugh. Someday, you'll be reminiscing about the simple days of sending text messages, and younger people will roll their eyes when you talk about Instagram and Twitter.

Before all this incredible technology, we talked to each other. That's what this book is about—relationships. Uno is a connector. He loves people. He wants to connect with them on a mental, emotional, and spiritual level. Uno simply wants to help. That pretty much describes me. I want to connect with and understand people. I want to help. I believe that's why I chose to be here, on this planet, in this body, during this exciting time in the spiritual evolution of humankind. That's also why I choose to stay plugged into Facebook—to connect, to love, to inspire, and to know a higher truth, despite the "human" appearances of separation and division.

The problems and challenges that Uno helps people overcome are familiar to all—fear, judgment, a sense of separation, people pleasing, grief, ill health, shame, challenging relationships, lack and limitation. Uno knows a higher truth. The 14 years I've spent studying New Thought's ancient spiritual ideas has led me to a rudimentary understanding of truth, and I try to keep it simple. It's based in love.

In a sense, this book is a reflection of the challenges I've faced over the years, and how Spirit has led me to a higher truth. I traveled through a dark period in my life last year, and because of the spiritual counseling I received, I emerged a different person— a new and improved version of myself. I love myself more and understand my mind better. I'm grateful to Spirit, and several people who loved me back to sanity. Again, love.

I know you will enjoy this book. I originally envisioned it as a book containing hundreds of truth affirmations, and nothing more. Then came Uno. Now that I think about it, that dog dream changed my life. It definitely changed this book. As I wrote it, I cried at times—not just because an innocent dog was pulling on my heartstrings. I cried because I was so grateful to be alive. I cried because Spirit was touching my heart as Uno was helping or loving someone. I predict you'll experience the same tears. I know you and I are "One" like that.

Mark Reed
March 2020

Chapter 1
Uno's Entrance

Thunder rumbled and rippled across the dark sky the night Uno was born. The storm was building slowly, sneaking up on the town—like a cat creeping up on a bird. Slowly and stealthily at first, and then BAM, a downpour, growling thunder, and flickers of lightning. Other than the impending rainfall, it was an ordinary summer evening in Macomb, Illinois. The year was 1976, and life was easy going for folks in this small Midwestern college town. Macomb wasn't a one-traffic-light town. The population was about 20,000, plus another 10,000 when Western Illinois University was in session. It was a nice-sized community with a town square, six grammar schools, one junior high and a high school, and twenty or so bars and taverns. All those college students from Chicago brought gobs of money and energy into

Macomb, but it was as dead as your great-great-granddaddy in the summer.

On this particular dark summer evening, kids were racing back home on their bikes for supper, legs pumping swiftly, desperate to beat the rain. Moms were busy in the kitchen, frying chicken and baking meatloaves, peering out their windows occasionally to keep an eye on the dark clouds. Dads were putting their tools back in the shed, as all responsible handymen do with rain on the horizon. Some were already napping on the couch, the sound of a Cardinals or Cubs game drifting from the adjacent family room.

For Uno's mother, a lazy nap on a couch would have been heaven. The four-year-old Golden Retriever was in cruel pain. She was a stray, and this would be her third litter in as many years, so she knew what to do. Her labor had started, instinct energized her, and she finally found a dry, secluded spot behind an enormous pile of scrap wood in the rear corner of the Hanan & Graham lumberyard on Lafayette Street. The rusted tin roof overhead kept her dry as the rain began to fall. She listened intently for the sound of humans or predators, but all sound washed away as the rain came down heavier, sounding like machine-gun fire on the tin roof. She circled in the dirt, pawing at it, building her birth nest. She lay down and groaned in pain.

Later in his life, Uno remembered the sound of that rain on the tin roof. He had distinct memories of the crashing thunder, the slime, the ooze, the wailing wind, and the stark glare of the world. He remembered his mother licking him incessantly and his two sisters, crying and squirming. Hours later, his mother was exhausted, dog-tired so to speak. Everyone slept soundly, warm, safe, and loved.

For weeks, Uno's life behind the scrap woodpile was exciting. So many sounds—people, machines, banging, crashing, and clattering. Uno and his sisters stayed close to mom, suckling and napping amid all the noise. At night, when it was silent, except for the chirping of the crickets, Uno and his sisters explored the lumberyard, never straying too far from that northwest corner. Their mother was always on guard, listening, corralling, prodding, and pacing. She would disappear for hours and return with scraps of food for Uno and his sisters after they grew tired of her milk. Life was comfortable, full of curiosity, and potential.

"Hey, look, Rich, a puppy!"

Before Uno knew what was happening, he was scooped up by an 8-year-old boy. Dave held him high in the air so his friend could inspect him.

"Wow, that is one cute pup!" shouted his friend, Rich.

Dave ran quickly to his bike. The boy was sure his mom would let him keep this poor little puppy. After all, it was abandoned, all alone in a lumberyard. He threw Uno over his shoulder as he mounted his Stingray. Uno was terrified and wriggling. "Let me go! Put me down!" he thought. He stretched his neck to see over the boy's shoulder. "There she is!" Uno saw his mother and sisters looking straight at him, eyes wide. It was the last time he ever saw his family.

Dave placed Uno in the front basket of his bicycle, in a canvas bag marked Macomb Daily Journal, and threw the bag's flap over Uno to make sure he didn't fall out of the basket. Ten minutes later, Uno was being held high in the air again, as Dave's mother looked at him with sympathetic eyes.

"Yes, he's adorable, but you know what your father said, you can't have a dog until you're ten years old."

"But mom!"

"No. You agreed with him, no dogs for another year and a half. Now I want you to take that dog back where you found him."

"Mahhhhhhm!"

"No, now go! Hurry, before it starts raining!"

Dave was heartbroken, but that's the answer he expected. He knew better than to argue with his father about a dog. The boy placed Uno back in his basket and pedaled the eight blocks back to the lumberyard. Uno was still in shock, trembling with fear. The lumberyard had closed by this time, so Dave placed Uno on the sidewalk near the front door.

"Good luck to you, boy. Wish I coulda kept ya." Dave hopped on his bike and sped away. The entire terrifying episode was over, like a bad dream. But where was his mom? Where were his sisters? Uno didn't recognize any of these surroundings. He curled up on a piece of grass near the entrance and waited. He waited and waited and waited.

It was getting dark now, and Uno didn't know where to go. Should he keep waiting or look for some water? He was so thirsty and wanted his mom so badly. For the first time in his life, Uno felt loneliness. Like a child in a store who suddenly realizes mom has vanished, Uno was all alone and didn't know what to do. He couldn't help it, he cried. Uno let out a long, wailing, high-pitched sob. "I want my mommy! Where is she?"

Just then, a towering figure rounded the sidewalk, and a pair of hands reached down for Uno.

"Hi, there! Oh, aren't you adorable? Was that you crying? Where's your mother?" The woman held Uno to her face and then looked around. She tucked Uno under her arm and walked a few feet to the door of the lumberyard. She stood there looking at the door and then knocked. No response. She walked a few feet to the right, then the left, and then held Uno up to her face again.

"Well, I don't know who you belong to, sweetie, but we can figure that out later. For now, you're coming with me. I'll be damned if I'm leaving you out here all night."

Thirty minutes later, Uno was gobbling up some type of strange food. It was soft and chewy and had a strong, musky smell to it. He devoured it, and she kept piling more of it in the bowl in front of him. Uno eagerly lapped up the water in the adjacent bowl. He was in heaven and getting so full.

He waddled from the kitchen into the woman's warm living room. She took a seat on a long, light blue sofa, put her feet up on the coffee table, and looked at Uno.

"Come on, boy," she said as she patted her lap. Uno tried to jump up on the couch several times but couldn't make it. The woman laughed, reached down, picked him up, and placed him on the sofa next to her. Uno had never felt anything so soft and comfortable. He looked up at the woman and smiled.

"If you belong to somebody, I'd like to kick their butt for being so irresponsible. But I don't think you do because you're not wearing a collar. Let's just say you found a forever home. How's that sound?" Uno gave Deb a blank stare. "I'm glad you agree.

Okay then, it's settled. You and I are gonna be best buds." The woman picked Uno up, held him to her face, and sweetly said, "Hi, I'm Deb. Nice to make your acquaintance. I'm going to love you like you've never been loved." Uno licked Deb's nose, and she scrunched up her face, laughing.

"Let's see. What are we gonna call you?" Deb laid her head back on the sofa pillow for a minute, thinking. "Hmmm, how about Woody, since I found you at the lumberyard?" Deb peered at Uno. "No, that won't do. I knew a Woody in high school, and he was a real nimrod. I don't wanna think of him every time I say your name." Deb laughed loudly. Uno cocked his head. "I know! How about Uno? The one and only, flying solo at the lumberyard. How's that sound, Uno?" Uno looked at Deb and tried to smile. He was still thinking of his mom. He hung his head low and whimpered.

"Oh you, come here." Deb picked up Uno and lay down on her side, curling into a ball with Uno cradled between her legs and belly. "My widdle Uno," she kept whispering as she stroked his back and head. Uno whimpered, and snuggled closer to her.

That night, as Uno lay in bed with Deb, he had an astonishing, awe-inspiring dream. It was one of those epic dreams, an all-night adventure. He dreamed that spirits from another world came to him. They silently hovered over him, and then he felt a jolt in his body like one of the spirits thumped his head. He woke up abruptly. The experience was surreal. He fell asleep again immediately and dreamed he was a beggar in ancient Mesopotamia, then a priest in Egypt, then a disciple of the philosopher Plotinus, a farmer in China, and a warrior in Mongolia. It was a very realistic dream with sights, sounds, and smells, and seemed to last forever. When Uno awoke the next morning, something was different.

Uno looked around. Deb was sleeping, gently snoring. It was quiet, the sun gently peeking into the window, and he heard the most beautiful birdsong.

"Where am I?" he thought. "Who am I?"

That second question was like an elbow in his ribs. "Why am I asking myself who I am?" He looked down and saw his paw.

"Holy Cow!" Uno jumped up to a standing position. He felt his tail wag. "I have a tail? What the hell?!"

Uno leapt off the bed, crashing and rolling on the soft carpet below. He ran to the full-length mirror standing next to Deb's dresser and stood in front of it, completely shocked. The world seemed to move in slow motion and then stood still. The next minute lasted an hour. Uno couldn't believe what he was seeing. "I'm a dog," he thought. He let that idea sink in for a minute. Again, he thought, "I'm a dog. No, I'm a puppy. How can this be?" He stood there, just looking at himself in the mirror and then squatted down.

In that instant, something shifted within Uno's mind. It felt like a sudden and decisive click in his consciousness, like a light switch turning on. He knew! He knew who he was. "Yes, I'm a dog," he thought. "But I have been so much more. All those people I was dreaming about, they were me. I was them." Suddenly, a rush of memories like a raging river flooded his mind.

Then it happened. Whoosh! Uno awakened! His consciousness expanded! His mind became lucid and unencumbered.

He remembered all his past lives, instantly. They rushed through his mind like a speeding train. He remembered existing in the universe in complete bliss, what some people might call the afterlife. He recalled teaching others in another realm. He remembered feeling at one with the universe, floating through the cosmos. These memories seemed to span millions of years, but he intuitively knew that time wasn't real. He sensed that he had lived as all those people, in all those places, but was experiencing these lives here in the present moment, all at once. Uno grew confused and dizzy and had to squat down again.

He remembered the Law of the Universe. When a soul reincarnates, temporary mental blindness shields them from remembering past lives, while retaining those memories in the One Mind of the universe. A human infant's mind is a blank slate. He knew this law. This certainty was more than intuition—he knew it. "So why?" he asked himself. "Why do I remember all these past lives? Why is this happening? Why am I here, in the body of a dog?"

Uno sat in front of the mirror for an hour, thinking, pondering, and waiting for an answer to come. Nothing did. So he walked to the empty food bowl that Deb placed in the corner of the bedroom, squatted, and waited for Deb to wake up. "Hurry up, Deb," he thought, "All this excitement has made me hungry!"

Chapter 2
Here's to Your Health

For the next several days, Uno spent his time in quiet contemplation. He was in mental observation mode, still growing accustomed to his crazy existence as a dog. Scores of memories continued to flash through his mind—images of past lives he'd lived in ancient Turkey, Egypt, Mesopotamia, India, and China. Some of these memories overwhelmed him; many had strong emotions attached to them. He finally decided to put them aside and focus on the here and now. It's easy to miss what's right in front of you when continually focusing on the past.

Deb was a kind and loving soul. Uno estimated she was in her early fifties, but she had the energy of a 30-year-old. She was a bit plump, some might say curvy, with large hips and a big bottom. Her dark brown hair was streaked with wisps of gray and was thick and curly. She had an oval-shaped face with the slightest double chin and a dimple on her right cheek that puckered when she smiled. Her full, encouraging smile is what drew your eyes to her face. There was something in her essence that was so familiar to Uno.

Deb danced and bopped through the house while doing her chores. Uno enjoyed sitting on the couch and watching her as she vacuumed, dusted, or folded the laundry. Deb would invariably stop whatever she was doing at any moment, strike a dramatic pose, and break out into song. "Stop, in the name of love!" She adored Motown music.

Deb included Uno in whatever she was doing. She loved to play records on the massive wooden 1960s-era stereo/radio system sitting in the corner of the living room. She preferred the Supremes, Temptations, Marvin Gaye, Mary Wells, and Gladys Knight and the Pips. Deb would slap a record on, grab Uno by his front paws, and dance around the living room. "Come on, boy, let's dance!" she would say as she laughed wildly over the music. Uno would break free of her grasp, jump straight up in the air several times, and run around her in circles until he got dizzy. When not dancing, he would just sit on the couch and watch her in wide amazement. Deb was fun, filled with positive energy, and it was apparent she had fallen in love with Uno.

A few weeks later, Deb installed a doggy door in the laundry room, leading out to the back yard. "Go on, boy, ain't no chains on you," she laughingly said as she used her foot to scoot Uno closer to the door. Uno looked up at her and flashed his happy smile. Deb laughed.

Uno crept haltingly through the doggy door, and when he felt that fresh summer morning air, he shot through. "Ah, freedom," he thought. "It's great to have in-and-out privileges." Deb had grown adept at noticing Uno's "gotta pee whimper," but he was relieved knowing he could exit and enter at will. Uno dawdled and diddled around the back yard, exploring all the crevices and future hidey-holes. The grass smelled delightfully fresh, and there was a slight breeze carrying a mixture of odors. In the back of the lot was a raised garden full of tomato plants, various gardening tools, a wheelbarrow, and an old, rusted swing set. The chains of the swing set hung low and swayed with the wind, searching for its long-lost seats. "Thank God, there's no fence," thought Uno.

Uno ventured into the neighbor's back yard just as old man Welker hobbled out of his back door. "Well, hello there, Uno!" he exclaimed gleefully. "Deb told me about you. My, my, aren't you a handsome young fella?" Uno looked up to the kindly looking man and wagged his tail. Mr. Welker was in his early eighties, mostly bald, and slightly hunched. His eyes glowed with kindness, and his broad smile accentuated his new dentures.

"Deb said I could invite you into my place, Uno, and I have some leftover ham that I don't want. My daughter still thinks I like ham," he chuckled. Mr. Welker walked into his house, turned around, and whistled to Uno. "Come on, boy!" Uno didn't hesitate. "I love ham," Uno thought.

"Whoa," thought Uno, "I feel like I've been transported back to the 1940s. Check out this kitchen." Mr. Welker had been living in his 1,700 square-foot Dutch colonial-style house since it was built in 1925, over 50 years now. Except for a 10-year-old refrigerator, the kitchen looked the same as it did when he re-modeled it back in '46 or '47. Mr. Welker plopped the piece of ham steak on a plate and placed it on the green and yellow-speckled linoleum floor. Uno dug in. Mr. Welker stood there and chuckled, watching him eat. "My goodness, you are hungry, huh? Doesn't Deb feed you?" Mr. Welker let out a funny sounding high-pitched squeal of a laugh as he loaded the plate with two more pieces of ham.

Uno ate too fast. He felt like he was going to be sick. He walked out of the kitchen, onto the woolly gold shag carpet in the living room and lay down next to a sofa. "I need to lie down," thought Uno. Mr. Welker joined him in the living room, taking a seat in a large green recliner next to the sofa. As he leaned back, Uno heard the click-click-click sound of the recliner and looked up.

"Are you going to take a nap there, Uno?" asked Mr. Welker. "Go ahead. I might take one too."

Mr. Welker picked up a book from the small table next to the recliner and began reading. Within a few minutes, the book was on his chest, and he was snoozing. His snoring sounded like a wounded wheeze. Uno's ears perked up, and he stood, gazing at Mr. Welker. "Something was wrong," Uno thought.

Uno slowly climbed up on the recliner and into Mr. Welker's lap, lying on his chest and knocking the book to the floor. Mr. Welker continued to wheeze. "He's sick," thought Uno. "But how do I know this?" Again, Uno felt something shift within his mind. It was a knowingness, a strong feeling. He pictured Mr. Welker in his mind and saw images of a hospital room, a nurse, and family members. He heard the word chemotherapy. "This is not the future," Uno thought. "It's the past. It was two days ago. The big 'C.' His daughter and son are terrified. Mr. Welker is fearful, and yet, not." Uno was curious about why these images were flashing through his mind.

"This man needs to heal," thought Uno. "He wants to heal." Uno felt this desire strongly.

Suddenly, Uno felt a massive surge of energy in his mind, within his entire being. He inched his way up and rested his head on Mr. Welker's neck. Uno closed his eyes, breathed deeply, and mentally centered himself with Universal Source Energy—the Infinite Intelligence. Uno began to pray affirmatively.

"I know the truth of this man," Uno thought. "I know Mr. Welker is whole, perfect, and complete exactly as he is. He lacks absolutely nothing to be the complete being that he is."

Mr. Welker's breathing slowed and became more relaxed.

Uno continued. "I know for Mr. Welker that every cell in his body is healing, bathed in the pure healing light of love, which is life itself. I know for him that any appearance of sickness and disease is not part of his reality. Any mutated cell or foreign agent in his body dissolves and dissipates under the power of this healing energy. I know this divine force, which is a perfect energy pattern, heals every cell and molecule in his body. It renews, reinvigorates, and reestablishes life. I know for Mr. Welker that he releases and lets go of any thought or belief related to pain, sickness, disease, or lack and limitation. I know for him that he is a perfect expression of harmony and balance—body, mind, and spirit. Healing, healing, healing, RIGHT NOW!"

A tear ran down Uno's cheek. He felt such an emotional release in this spiritual moment he was having, and he knew his truth-speaking was complete. He licked his lips in satisfaction.

Mr. Welker smiled as he continued napping, and his snores grew louder.

Here are a few **truth affirmations** and random thoughts related to *health*. They are written in the first-person voice just for you and are "Uno-approved."

- Perfect health is who and what I am.
- I have complete harmony of body, mind, and spirit.
- Every cell in my body dances with health and delight.
- Spirit's healing light is constantly and continuously healing my body and mind.
- Every day, and in every way, I am healing, healing, and healing.
- I know the truth about me—I am a perfect soul. Wholeness and perfection radiate through my body.
- Perfect health is my birthright based on who I am as a divine being.
- Healing energy rushes and vibrates through my body, healing everything in its path.
- My heart beats with dynamic love, animating every cell with love.
- My body is a perfect vessel of universal light and love.
- The universe longs to heal my body and mind.
- Spirit's healing love is forever renewing me.
- As life courses through me, it heals and animates my body.
- My vibrant health is assured based on my Oneness with Spirit.
- I am in the flow of life, and the flow of life is within me.
- My source is a divine fountain of life rushing through me.
- Goodness flows through me and expresses as dynamic health.
- I am inseparably connected to and synchronized with life.
- Every cell in my body is titillating with vigorous energy.
- I am free from the shackles of belief in sickness. I am life, I am health.
- I embrace the magnificent truth within—vigor, energy, well-being.
- I align myself with the truth of my being—wholeness and perfection.

- My wholeness enlightens any appearance of sickness.
- I lift my gaze above any sense of limitation and open my mind to the Allness of the universe.
- I am in excellent health. Every cell in my body is healthy and whole.
- I am the revelation of wholeness.
- I breathe Spirit in, I breathe Spirit out.
- Every cell, fiber, tissue, and organ of my body is healed, NOW!
- The greatest Healer of all is where I am right now.
- Every cell in my body is happy and healthy!
- Wholeness is my birthright. Therefore, I stand in the awareness that every cell, every organ, and every function of my being is vibrating at a high vibration with vigor and vitality. I am immersed in this truth, right here, right now.
- My body, made from Universal Divine Intelligence, knows how to heal itself.
- I see complete health in my body, mind, and spirit. Only love flows through me.
- Divine Wisdom is running through every cell of my body.
- The health of God is expressing in me, through me, and as me. I am the very health of God.
- Every cell in my body sings at the frequency of the Divine.

Rhyming Affirmations

I am healthy, whole, and complete,
From the top of my head to the toes on my feet.

Every cell in my body is singing and dancing,
When my body needs healing, I give it some romancing.

My body has an intuitive knowledge and ability to heal,
Sexy is subjective, but my body definitely has health appeal.

My body responds to my healing thoughts,
Vibrant health is what I gots.

I am perfect balance and harmony—body, spirit, and mind,
God is right there, infusing, intermingling, intertwined.

I am Spirit in expression, a mini-me of God,
I focus on love and I heal my bod.

Divine Love flows through me and expresses as vibrant health,
Not just a state of well-being, but a thriving commonwealth.

Wholeness is my birthright, a divine provision,
Nurturing this completeness is my decision.

I embrace the truth of my being—health, energy, and vigor,
As I pray upon this truth, it gets bigger and bigger.

I have a clean bill of health, like my bathtub ducky,
To think less of myself would make me feel yucky.

Uno's Random Thoughts

A professor placed two glasses of water on the stage. She split the class of 100 in two, asking 50 students to send thoughts of love to the water in glass #1 and asking the other half of the class to send thoughts of hate to glass #2. The class did this for 5 minutes. Later, drops of water from both glasses were placed under a microscope. The water molecules from glass #1 (love) looked like normal water. The water molecules from glass #2 (hate) looked fragmented, mutated, and jagged. Thoughts have power over the physical world.

We have no problem believing that a hypochondriac can adversely affect his or her health by continually thinking of pain, sickness, and disease. Why do we have trouble believing the opposite?

Our bodies are the vehicle carrying our souls. The body is neither good nor bad, constructive or destructive, right or wrong. Bodies are just bodies. But our thoughts can be constructive or destructive and can heal or harm the body. The mind "causes." The body is just an effect.

Our healing powers are our birthright, given to us by Spirit. We are naturally creative beings, made in the likeness of our Creator. We can use our creative ability to heal a stubbed toe or cancer, there is no difference. The only limits to our power are those we hold in our minds. As Jesus said, "It is done unto you as you believe."

Chapter 3
F.E.A.R.—Face Everything and Relax

"Being a dog has its perks," thought Uno several weeks later.

"Everyone loves me, I can smell the cookies as soon as they start baking in the oven, and I don't have a job."

"Well, I guess I do have a job in this incarnation," he thought. "I'm still trying to figure it out."

Uno rolled over on his side and came face to face with Deb on the bed. Her nostrils softly whistled as she breathed. His face was inches from hers, and he could see the sun reflecting on the drool running down the corner of her mouth. It must be close to wakey-wakey time because his stomach was starting to murmur.

A minute later, Uno's stomach growled like a wounded tiger. "Sorry, Deb, but you need to wake up," he thought. Uno leaned in toward Deb and licked her face repeatedly. Her eyes fluttered, and her head rolled to avoid his wet tongue. Nothing. This time, he went for her ear, slathering it with love saliva. "Wakey wakey, Deb!" he thought as he laughed to himself. Deb's hand slid between his tongue and her head.

"Uno, stop," she croaked. Deb turned her head back toward Uno and opened her eyes.

"You are a pain, son," she grumbled. "Is it chow time?"

"Woohoo! She used the 'chow' word!" Deb knew that HE knew that word. Uno whimpered.

"All right, all right," whispered Deb. "Let's go. Chow time."

Later that afternoon, Uno could hear the Miller family arguing next door. Again. Still.

"Sometimes," he thought, "this super canine hearing I possess isn't much of a perk. It's nice when I can hear the mailman walking up the steps, or when I'm upstairs and Deb pours that hard, chunky dog food in my metal bowl down in the kitchen— but sometimes it's a nuisance. Humans have no idea what it's like to have a kajillion sounds constantly poking at their ears.

"The Miller family," thought Uno. "Not a big family, just a mom and dad in their '30s and their 8-year-old daughter, Crystal. Cute as a kitten, that one."

"They love to argue, and they're loud," thought Uno. "Competing and 'being right' is like an Olympic sport for them." Uno imagined that the couple's parents routinely shushed them when they were children, and now they were doing their best to make up for it.

Uno heard the Millers arguing intermittently throughout the day as he lay in the back yard watching the birds. Their quarrels were oddly amusing. The laundry was folded incorrectly (it seems Mrs. Miller can't do anything right). Mr. Miller needs to change three light bulbs, and if he doesn't, he's getting turnip soup for dinner. Mrs. Miller acts too much like her irritating mother (a few swear words followed that one). Crystal is hiding in her room again and needs to make some new friends. Mr. Miller needs to get off his butt and find a better-paying job in Macomb, but the damn town is too small. On and on and on.

Later that evening, as Deb laughed loudly at the television, Uno wandered over to the Miller's house. Crystal slept in the basement. She begged her parents for weeks to let her move into the large room on the north side of the house. The basement temperature was slightly cooler than Crystal's upstairs bedroom during the summer, so her parents finally obliged. Purple was her favorite color—a purple bedspread, a thick purple rug, a purple stuffed unicorn, and a large, purple-colored poster of David Cassidy on the wall over her bed.

Uno grinned as he watched Crystal lying on her bed. The small window on the wall opposite her bed afforded Uno the perfect spot to gaze down on this precious angel. She was different from her parents—quiet and always smiling. Uno loved to creep up to that window whenever he heard music wafting from next door. Like most kids her age, Crystal preferred what they were calling "bubblegum" music—David Cassidy, Donny Osmond, The Jackson Five, Bobby Sherman, The Archie's. She had a habit of dancing around her room, a hairbrush in her hand that she used as a microphone. Uno loved this girl.

But there was no dancing tonight. Crystal was crying, curled up in a ball on her bed. Her sobbing pierced Uno's heart. He cried with her. A minute later, Uno couldn't take any more. He scratched the window glass.

Crystal's head jerked up, and she looked around the room. Uno continued scratching. She turned her head to the window and saw Uno. A broad smile replaced the scowl on her face, and she quickly wiped the tears from her face with the bedspread.

"Uno!" she cried out. Yes, she knew Uno. Everyone knew Uno.

She ran across the room, climbed on a small table, and unlatched the window. Uno crept closer to her. Crystal reached out, grasped Uno's midsection, and pulled him through the window. She held him there for a moment as Uno licked her face furiously.

"Hi, Uno!" she giggled as she cradled him in her arms and carried him to the bed. "What are you doing here? What a nice surprise! You know, you can come to visit me anytime you want."

Uno and Crystal lay on their sides facing each other while Crystal told Uno all about her life. Her school science project, her friend, Amber, who experienced her first kiss, the annoying boy who was always watching her during recess, Uno got an ear full. He smiled at Crystal and listened intently. She finally ran out of energy and leaned back on the giant purple pillow behind her head. Crystal was content, Uno was a good listener. She continued looking at Uno in silence and then dozed off, a smile on her face.

Uno crept closer to Crystal and rested his head on her hands, folded near her head. "As much as she tries to hide it, this darling girl is in pain," Uno thought. He felt her oppressive thoughts. She had talked about everything in her life except her parents. But Uno could hear them in her mind.

Arguments. Name calling. Anger. Mean spiritedness. Frustration. Confusion. Uno could feel it all. Crystal's thoughts and feelings were a tangled mess, like a spider web of gnarled and knotted electrical wires.

Uno heard the word "divorce" in her mind. He felt her fear deep in his soul—abandonment, betrayal, withdrawal, loneliness, terror.

Uno had heard the Millers talk about many things, but never divorce. But in the mind of a child, darkness creates its own monsters. Our self-inflicted fears and worries often overshadow reality. Crystal was afraid—not just fearful of an imagined divorce, but also about not fitting in at school, about her math grades, about boys, and about all the little things in life she couldn't control. Her fear thoughts were slapping her around. "She has no idea how perfect, innocent, and safe she is," thought Uno.

He closed his eyes and focused all his energy on this beautiful, pure, God-presence lying before him.

"I know for Crystal that she is absolutely and divinely perfect. She is whole and complete just as she is—pure innocence. I know for her that she releases all fear from her mind, and an indescribable and embracing love replaces her dark thoughts. She loves herself completely. She loves her parents wholly and knows that they love her unconditionally and unreservedly. Crystal feels this love surrounding every thought and feeling in her mind, right here and now. I know for Crystal that she envisions herself and her parents cuddled and canoodled in a love bubble. Nothing can touch Crystal in this bubble. She feels nothing but love. I call upon a legion of souls to watch over her and strengthen and reinforce this love bubble all the days of her life. Crystal is completely at peace as she rests in this love, content as a baby in her mother's adoring arms. This is Crystal's truth. I know it beyond all doubt."

Uno relaxed deeper into Crystal's mind. He crept closer, resting his snout on Crystal's smiling face. He loved her deeply and could feel this love coursing through her mind.

Here are a few **truth affirmations** and random thoughts related to being *fearless and self-loving*. They are written in the first-person voice just for you and are "Uno-approved."

- I release and let go of all fears, knowing they are simple misperceptions.
- Love washes away any limiting thoughts in my mind.
- I love myself. I am kind and gentle with myself.
- Self-love, fueled by God within, guides my thoughts and actions.
- I am fearless and so I love more.
- All that I desire, I already am.
- I am brave and courageous. I stand strong and love myself.
- All of life supports me in everything I think, say, and do.
- I am divinely supported, always.
- My confidence grows and expands as I leave fear behind.
- I scrape off the fear from my mind and wash it with love.
- I look fear directly in the eyes and know it's not real. Love is real, and I am love.
- God is more powerful than this, and I am an expression of God.
- I boldly embrace my inner light and let it shine on myself and others.
- I trust myself. I embrace myself. I love myself.
- I grow through all the experiences I go through.
- The faith and love I have for myself are powered by God, and it is good.

- I am the strength, courage, and passion that stands firmly in love.
- I am powered by a Loving, Universal Intelligence that guides me to love myself more and more each second.
- I trust the Loving Voice within and listen to it always.
- I walk out of the cave of darkness, and I see nothing but love. I love myself, dearly.
- The love, power, and strength that is within my mind flush away all false and limiting thoughts.
- I see only love. I have love, I give love, I am love.
- I am not my past; I am what I choose to be now.
- I am surrounded by love, immersed in peace, and strengthened by God.
- Fear is a mirage. The love I feel for myself is real.
- I love myself, and I share my love with all.
- I release any fear thoughts, knowing they are all make-believe. I love myself, knowing I am blessed.
- I have found a place of sublime peace and blissful love. It is here, within me.
- I am safe and secure in the loving inner embrace of God.
- False and limiting thoughts are unwanted visitors. God and I own my mind.
- I choose love over fear and strength over limitation.
- The love I have for myself is my pillow. I rest, knowing I am safe and secure.
- I let go of all that I thought I was and embrace love, peace, and strength.
- I am self-confident because I have a loving power supporting and guiding me.
- I acknowledge fear, I hear it, but I know it's not real. God is real, I am real.
- I let go of the false idea that life can go wrong, and I know that my life is right—right now, right here.
- I expect nothing but good in my life because I am good.
- I am devoted to my peace and happiness.

- Love is my priority. I let everything else go.
- I am awake and aware. I know fear is simply part of the dream world.
- I laugh at fear's powerlessness. I am powered by God.
- Love is my home. I am home now.
- I have the courage to face anything. I embrace courage. I am courageous.
- I love myself so much that I see no fear.
- Fear and doubt are dark clouds. My self-love is the shining sun.
- I am pure light, I am love, I am powerful, I am.
- I am one with all the love the universe provides.
- When I am temporarily not seeing correctly, love takes my hand and guides me. Always.
- I stop creating drama in my mind. I create love, I accept love, I am love.
- I am committed to my self-growth and self-love.
- I am swimming in the flow of life. Love uplifts me, and I float in peace.
- I am free from all negative and limiting thoughts. Love is my source and supply.
- I put my trust in God, I am a creation of God, I have faith in myself.
- My heart is made of peace, and my mind is formed from love.
- I surrender all fear, doubt, uncertainty, and any thought of separation. I am one with God, one with love, and one with myself.

Rhyming Affirmations

Fear is not real, I cut it out with a knife.
Love heals all, love is my life.

Love has my back, fear is a mutation,
I hear the voice of love and know it's my foundation.

Fear goes poof when I practice gratitude,
Love is the bedrock of my daily attitude.

When fear knocks on the door, I say, "hello, now go away,"
My self-love expands as I meditate and pray.

Fear is a lie, living only in my mind,
Love is for real; I am entirely aligned.

I love myself, I am not afraid,
Love is for real; fear is the charade.

My mind is a palace, no longer a slum,
Love replaces fear, and I overcome.

Today I choose peace and let go of fear,
I know all is well, right now, right here.

I ask, I know, I affirm, I believe,
I am more than worthy, and I receive.

Fear is a flimsy veil that I walk right through,
I search my mind and know what is true.

Uno's Random Thoughts

Fear is like a shadow. It's dark, and it may look large, but it's not real. It's a reflection of my thoughts, but it's not who I am.
Fear exists only in my mind, and if there's one thing I can change, it's my mind.

Fear is something we must walk through, not avoid. When we see our fears for what they are, they look fragile and feeble. We know fear has no real power.

Superstitions are just plain silly. Fear is the foundation of superstition. How can we trust a feeling that's the basis of something so daffy and dopey? Turn away from fear as you would a fool. Don't give it your valuable mental energy.

When we face our fears and move beyond them, we discover a new freedom. We do this by learning to immediately identify fear in our mind, see it for what it is, and let it go.

Chapter 4
Judgment is For Giving Up

“Deb must be going somewhere," thought Uno. She's getting ready to ride that old bicycle.

Deb was in the driveway behind her Carroll Street home prepping "Old Red," the 1960s-era bicycle she bought at a garage sale several years ago. Old Red was a relic—it was a girl's 26-incher with thick tires, a 3-speed gearbox that no longer worked, wide handlebars, and a monster seat—perfect fit for a 50-something-year-old woman's widening backside. Deb spray-painted it fire engine red to cover the rust and mounted a large basket in front. The cherry on top was a ching-ching-ching bell ringer near the handlebar grip. She laughed every time she used it.

"Come on, boy! We're going for a little ride!" Deb scooped up Uno and secured him in the basket, a comfortable old blanket beneath him.

"I'm not sure about this at all," thought Uno. "God, please let her be a safe driver."

Deb lunged forward and pushed down hard on the right pedal. The bike wobbled precariously because of Uno's weight in the basket, but she steadied the handlebars and regained balance. Deb shouted, "Here we go, boy!" Ching-ching-ching! She threw her head back and laughed like a crazy woman.

Deb was a veteran on a bicycle. She learned to ride when she was seven years old. Back in the 1930s, she and her friends explored every street and back alley of Macomb. She distinctly remembered her eighth birthday. Her dad bought her the best gift ever—a shiny, sky blue colored Schwinn Cycleplane. For a kid during the depression, that was the equivalent of owning a Corvette or Cadillac. "They don't make bikes like that anymore," thought Deb.

Past the First Presbyterian Church, left at the YMCA, Deb gained speed as she passed Aurelio's Pizzeria, her favorite pizza joint. She swore she could smell mushrooms and onions. Deb whizzed by the old train station, made a right at Swede's Auto Body, a left onto Adams Street, and made her final turn onto McArthur Street, where her brother Tim lived.

Tim and Deb grew up in the two-story brick house at 423 McArthur Street, and the old homestead contained a ton of memories for her. As she rolled into the driveway, Deb flashbacked to the summer of 1933, when she and Tim painted the house. They painted the lower half of the exterior a dark chocolate brown color. Deb called it "do-do brown" when she was eight, and Tim thought that was hilarious. But mom and dad forbade them from painting the upper half of the house because mom was scared to death of them falling off a ladder, so the original pale yellow remained. The entire house looked rather dim and weathered in 1976. It was definitely time for a new paint job. Deb and Tim were both in their fifties now, so this time they'd hire a few college students and paint the entire house.

When Deb walked into the house, Tim was in his usual spot—the blistered and faded dark leather comfy chair and wide matching ottoman in front of his Admiral color television set. It stood proudly in the corner—a light walnut color, with four wide legs that raised it a good eight inches off the floor. Its top surface was as shiny as it was on the day he bought it in 1965, at the Sears in Quincy, owing to Tim giving it a good Pledge shine every week. She remembered when he brought it home. He was so proud and excited to own a color TV and "finally see the world in color," as he said. Nowadays, he called it, "The Admiral," as in "I'm just sittin' here watchin' the Admiral."

Deb loved her older brother, dearly. They were close growing up, being only two years apart. Unlike other siblings she knew, they rarely argued. He had always been a wonderful big brother—protective, inclusive, and caring. Women his age would say Tim was a good-looking guy. He had thin, dark brown hair, most of it still on his head. He sported a neatly trimmed goatee surrounding a devious smile. But these days, Tim was not a happy man. He was about 50 pounds overweight, liked being single, and had a sour view of people, and the world in general.

Tim loved his sweets (and red meat, and potatoes, and pasta, and…) and got minimal exercise. He was bored and fatigued in his job at the McDonough County Clerk's office, which he'd endured, as he put it, for the last 28 years. He was respected in his job, and good at it, but was ready for retirement. He needed a new life, desperately. His days revolved around work, television, and walking his German Shepherd, Django. More than bored, he was angry all the time. He cursed at the TV, was constantly irritated about politics, and generally had a caustic attitude about life. It was apparent he didn't like himself much and projected that animosity onto the world.

"You'll never believe what President Ford is doing now!" he exclaimed when Deb walked into the living room.

"Unless he tripped and fell again, I don't care."

"Hey! Uno! Come here, buddy!"

After Uno and Django exchanged cursory sniffs, Uno jumped up in Tim's lap. Tim held him close to his face, and they exchanged kisses. Uno loved Tim too. How could you not? Despite his inner anger and sourness, he was a lovable guy. Uno knew he was a kind soul trapped in a gloomy life he'd created for himself.

"Why don't you take Uno for a walk? He's been doing nothing but laying around the house for the last couple of days." Deb chuckled to herself as she realized she could have been talking about Tim. "I'm going to work on your curtains today. The green ones need some stitch work."

"Eh, I don't know."

"Come on, get out of here. It's a beautiful day. Go talk to Jeff down at the Roe Boat. It's almost lunchtime."

Tim immediately thought of deep-fried mushrooms. "Yeah, okay, a little fresh air would be good, I guess. Right, Uno?" Uno looked up at Tim and smiled. Walking was always a good idea to Uno.

Uno loved the smell of grass, and the subtle aromas of his kindred canines on the several trees and bushes he and Tim passed by on their two-block walk to the Roe Boat. You can tell a person is kind when they're not constantly tugging on your leash during a walk. Tim was one of those people, so patient. As they crossed Adams Street, Tim could hear a group of children playfully screaming on the giant swing set at Grant Elementary School.

"Sit wherever you'd like, Tim," shouted Jeff, the bartender. Jeff did a double take. "Hey, Uno! You brought my favorite pooch, Tim. Does he want some beer or a whiskey sour today?"

"Ha ha, good one, Jeff," chuckled Tim. "No, Uno's on the wagon today." Both Jeff and Tim laughed.

It was early in the day. There were only three other people in Tim's favorite tavern and restaurant. Owned by Mr. Harold Roe, the Roe Boat was a fixture in Macomb—the best steaks, giant sandwiches, a great surf 'n turf, and a notorious pork tenderloin sandwich. The place was packed every Friday and Saturday night. It was small and softly lit, containing just 18 tables and booths, and a horseshoe-shaped bar seating eight. Uno's sensitive nose was filled with the lingering aromas of booze, cigarette smoke, fried food, and cooked beef. The uniformed waitresses whizzed down the aisles, grazing any overweight hips and thighs protruding from the cramped wooden booths. The Roe Boat was old school in appearance but had an upbeat and inviting personality.

"Hey, you brought Uno with you," Kay said with big eyes. "How's my widdle Uno?" Kay leaned down to pet him, and he furiously licked Kay's nose. She shrieked and giggled.

Kay was one of the Roe Boat's veteran waitresses. She was 40-something, had her permed blonde hair stacked high on her head, and always had a smile and kind word. Jeff, the bartender, liked to kid around with the waitresses, and especially with Kay, because she had a great sense of humor. He once spread a rumor that Flo, the waitress on the TV sitcom "Alice," was modeled after Kay. Several of the more gullible customers believed him.

Tim and Uno took a seat opposite each other in the dark corner booth near the bar. Tim had his usual—the giant Pork T sandwich and an order of deep-fried mushrooms. The Pork T was twice as large as the over-sized bun, jammed with grilled onions and pickles. Tim was in heaven. Uno looked on with big eyes, licking his chops. He knew what was in store. Tim broke off little pieces of the pork and dropped them on the small plate in front of Uno. Kay cackled as she watched Uno gobble up his lunch. "I think Uno likes our tenderloins more than you do, Tim!"

As Tim ate, he gazed off in the distance, deep in thought. Uno could hear those thoughts and "see" the images racing through his mind. Tim's thoughts always seemed so jumbled, shrouded in a kind of darkness—frustration, judgment, anger, fear. He held resentments against his supervisor and several co-workers, he disdained politicians, and had a general mistrust of all people, except his sister Deb. He loved his dog, Django, that was for sure. Tim loved all animals. That's how Uno knew he was a loving person, deep down. Uno had compassion for this man and knew that he could be so much happier if he only took control of his mind.

"Too many people in the world are similar," thought Uno. "They merely react to their thoughts instead of learning to control and use them to better their lives. They have no idea they were born to be mentally creative."

Uno knew that forgiveness was the key. He remembered this valuable spiritual practice from his past lives. During dozens of his lives, he had struggled with the idea of "letting go." Like Tim, the soul who inhabited Uno's furry body had been on the same emotional-spiritual consciousness level as most of his fellow earth dwellers—judgmental—always pointing a finger "out there," channeling the dislike he had for himself onto everyone else.

In the mid-14th century, the soul currently known as Uno, lived as a priest in Lyon, France. Thinking back, it was during this life that he learned the essence of genuine self-love. He heard the confession of hundreds of tortured souls, many of whom had made terrible mistakes. He referred to them as mistakes, not sins, because errors can be corrected. Sins are a judgment, a condemning finger created by humankind, pointed at humankind. Uno knew that the Loving Universal Intelligence doesn't point fingers. Humans judge humans based on their false and limiting belief systems. But it was during this life as a priest that he witnessed scores of people learning to forgive themselves. The lesson was clear: once a human's consciousness was free of darkness, they judged others less and were therefore happier.

Tim hadn't killed or tortured anyone, as many people had during those Renaissance times. The problems humans faced in the 20th century were fluffy marshmallows compared with the harsh and cruel struggles people endured back in the day. But Uno could hear Tim's mental obstacles—his thoughts—and they troubled Tim daily. He embraced these unwanted thoughts, returning to them often, as an alcoholic returns to the bottle. Uno could hear them—a girlfriend who abandoned him, backbiting and gossiping co-workers, a micro-managing supervisor, Richard Nixon and his gang of dishonest flunkies. In other words, typical issues most humans deal with in various forms.

On top of others' wrongdoing, Tim judged himself harshly—his past guilt and shame, his weight, his "perceived" lack of abilities, and a host of other false beliefs he carried around, like a backpack filled with heavy rocks. Tim needed to forgive himself and others if he was ever going to progress in this life. Spiritual growth was why Tim chose to reincarnate, even though he didn't remember this choice.

Uno mentally connected with Tim in that moment. As Tim sat there, staring off into space while eating, Uno planted these seeds into the One Mind:

"I know for Tim that he is a perfect creation of a Perfect Creator, sharing the same qualities and characteristics as his Maker. Tim also shares God's creative power, co-creating his reality by the thoughts he thinks and the beliefs he holds in consciousness. I know for Tim that he wipes clean the chalkboard of his mind. He releases all thoughts and beliefs that are misperceptions of truth—fear, anger, resentment, and judgment. He clears away thoughts of being 'less than' or 'better than.' He releases the divisive, dualistic ideas of 'right' and 'wrong.'"

"I know for Tim that he forgives others easily. He knows that all humans are doing the best they can with the understanding they have. He empathizes with others who make mistakes in life, who act in non-loving ways, who hurt others, who act selfishly. No matter what the errors are, great or small, Tim forgives others for their humanness. Tim forgives himself for any mistakes he has made. He sees his humanness clearly and loves himself for it. He knows he is a divine creation with a human personality and gives himself a break by allowing himself to embrace his errors in thinking. I know for Tim that he forgives himself for seeing others as separate from him. He lets go of all perceptions of evil and sees others as spiritual siblings, regardless of their actions. He understands the idea of 'spiritual sickness,' and like someone who has a physical dis-ease, he doesn't judge those who act out any type of spiritual illness they possess. As Tim's consciousness is cleared and wiped clean of all these misperceptions, he uses his conscious mind to plant new seeds into his subconscious mind. He speaks the truth of who he is—perfect, whole, and complete. He sees himself as loving, kind, and compassionate. He envisions a higher truth for himself and others. He listens to the Inner Loving Voice, his True Self—the voice that tells him that, like God, he is peace in expression, happy and joyful, and accepting of himself and all life forms. I know this to be the truth about Tim, and I give thanks for this truth channeling through me. I know my word has power and that this truth has no choice but to manifest in Tim's life exactly as I have planted it into the One Mind, which Tim shares. Thank you, Father, Mother, God."

Here are a few **truth affirmations** and random thoughts related to being *less judgmental and more forgiving and loving and accepting of life as it is*. They are written in the first-person voice just for you and are "Uno-approved."

- I forgive anyone and everyone for any past, present, or future perceived wrongdoing, and I forgive myself for my misperceptions of others.
- I release all expectations of others and myself.
- Peace flows through my mind and silences all false thoughts.
- Peace and serenity envelop my mind as I let go of any "shoulds."
- I am kind and gentle with myself.
- I let other people be who they are, not who I want them to be, and I feel peace.
- Contentment envelops me like a warm blanket. I release the world from my grip.
- I let go of any desire to be right.
- My heart leads me in all my relationships.
- A perfect stillness blankets my mind as I detach from the world.
- I detach from the world and love its inhabitants at the same time.
- I dispatch blessings to the world and its inhabitants as I disengage from expectations and judgments.
- I know I can exist peacefully with others. I have come here to do this, and I accept my role as a lover and supporter of others.
- I release any belief that other people should change.
- Everyone is exactly where they need to be, including me. I accept everyone and everything as it is.

- I plan the fishing trip but not the fish fry. I let go of all outcomes.
- I am adjusting my focus and seeing everyone as perfect—perfect as they are.
- I think before I speak. I harm no one, and I am guided by the inner voice of love.
- I am the reason someone smiles today. I project love to the world.
- I expect nothing, and I treasure everything.
- I know what is best for me. I listen within for the voice of wisdom.
- I expect all good things from the universe as I release expectations of people.
- I am persistent in loving myself and others.
- Gratitude surrounds me as I let go of all judgment.
- I let go of judging others by not judging myself.
- Forgivingness comes easily and effortlessly. I release all judgment.
- I give up judging others, and mentally surround myself with love.
- I deserve the peace I feel by not judging myself or others. I am worth it.
- I release all resistance to life by forgiving everyone and everything.
- I know everyone sees the world differently than I and accept this knowledge in my heart.
- I feel good about me when I let go of all judgments.
- Embracing a higher truth, I judge less and love more.
- I am free of all anger and resentment as I turn my attention away from the judging voice.
- I am optimistic about life and my fellow travelers. I see the good in all.
- I accept conflict as a part of life, and I see it for what it is.
- 20/20 vision is mine! I see the goodness in all.

- I am rich beyond imagination because I love others and myself.
- I see everyone's worth, knowing we all have something to offer the world.
- I let go of the foolish idea that I know better, and I accept the love and peace that results.
- I disconnect from the world and connect to a loving inner power.
- Gratitude and peace of mind are mine as I let go of any competition I feel with the world.
- I win peace by losing the desire to be right.
- Serenity and peace embrace me as I walk away from competition and the desire to be right.

Rhyming Affirmations

I give up defending,
and start befriending.

I release and let go of all expectation,
Inner peace is my new affirmation.

I have no desire to compete or be right,
My love is shining, and boy is it bright.

I give up judging, it just causes so much grief,
Love and acceptance is my new belief.

I accept myself as I am and everyone else too,
My outlook is peaceful, I see the world anew.

I have 20/20 vision, I see the good in all,
My inner peace was short, but now it's really tall.

I listen to the voice of wisdom, it comes from within,
I forgive myself for whatever, and lovingly begin again.

Forgiveness is letting go, it definitely works for me,
I collect the sweetness of life, like a little honeybee

I forgive, I let go, I release, I see,
A brand new world in front of me.

Everyone, everywhere has a different understanding,
I accept them as they are, and I feel outstanding.

Uno's Random thoughts

Each of us is in partnership with God, whether we know it or not. Not God as a person, but God as in life itself. What we call life energy, the animating force of the universe, is the same thing we call Universal or Agape Love. The universe is continually emanating love/life. When we judge others or ourselves, or refuse to forgive, we are acting unnaturally, and we experience the consequences—judgment, anger, resentment, guilt. When we are in alignment with love, we are in our natural state and experience more desirable consequences—inner peace, love, contentment, gratitude.

Every day, we hear a chorus of voices in the world telling us that we are separate and distinct from each other. We continuously walk through a gauntlet of meaningless and misguiding internal and external "tweets" trying to persuade us to judge each other. We must learn to ignore what the world and our own false and limiting beliefs tell us and listen to the voice of love within. God/Spirit needs your voice so It can help others. In truth, there are no "others," there is only the One. Spirit and all living creatures make up the One. Universal Spirit not only loves you, and wants you to be happy and at peace, It needs you to be a channel for its love. Like a three-legged race, we are all in this together.

Forgiveness is the key to happiness. The mind that does not forgive is full of fear and cannot be at peace. Forgiveness is a broad term encompassing every person, situation, action, thought, or belief that is out of alignment with universal and unconditional love. Ninety-nine percent of what we see, hear, experience, and think, requires us to forgive. Forgiveness is not just an act, but a constant state of mind that is powered by love, leading to peace.

Our beliefs forge the chains that bind us to unhappiness, anger, and fear—they are our own worst enemy. If we could eliminate all our beliefs, we would be at peace. God doesn't need our belief. God is God, and love is love. They simply are. Instead of believing in God, experience God. Instead of believing in love, embody and express love.

When I offer forgiveness to someone, I lower the drawbridge and invite that person into my castle. I "join" with that person, which is my purpose in life. Everything that unites us is of God, based in love.

Chapter 5
Knowing Your Own Truth is Numero Uno

It was a beautiful fall morning in Macomb, a crisp 46 degrees. Uno decided to walk himself since Deb was busy with a craft project. She and her quilting friends were having a get-together at Deb's house, and Uno hightailed it out of there. The idea of four women fawning over him all day long was unbearable.

As he walked, Uno thought, "Thank God my human senses are intact. I pray for the dogs and cats who don't know enough to look both ways before crossing." Anyone who was watching Uno that morning would find his safety sense a curious phenomenon. A 30-something-year-old jogger woman was both amused and puzzled when she witnessed Uno waiting patiently for the red light to turn green as he walked down Lafayette Street toward the town square.

On his walk toward the downtown area, Uno stopped at Chandler Park. This historic city block with crisscrossing brick sidewalks featured a statue of General Macomb, chiseled memorials of local war heroes, a genuine 19th-century cannon, an aging gazebo, playground, and plenty of fresh grass just waiting for Uno to cop a squat.

Uno approached a man sitting on a park bench. He had the kindest eyes. Uno recognized him. On several occasions, he'd spotted him walking around town. People called him "Chilly," although Uno didn't know why, or his actual name. The man was 60-ish, gray-haired, and balding. He wore a pair of faded overalls and a black and white-striped train engineer-type hat. Under his tattered brown leather jacket, an overall strap hung down by his side, revealing a dirty white t-shirt. He sported vintage black combat boots that looked like they hadn't seen a shine box since the late 50s.

"Well, hello there, Uno," he chirped.

"How does everyone know my name?" wondered Uno.

Chilly patted the seat on the park bench next to him. "Wanna join me, boy?"

Uno paused in front of Chilly, just staring at the man. He jumped up on the park bench, sat down facing Chilly, and gave him a big smile.

"My, my, you are a smart one." Uno widened his grin. Chilly reached over and gave Uno's head and ears a good scratch and rub.

"Yes, someone has taught you good manners, haven't they, boy?" Chilly extended his scratching down Uno's back to that sweet spot in front of his tail.

"Oh my God, that feels heavenly," thought Uno.

Chilly leaned back on the chipped and faded park bench, lit an unfiltered cigarette, took a bottle out from his hip pocket, and gave it three long chugs. He looked back at Uno, who was gazing off in the distance, his tongue hanging out. Chilly leaned back on the bench and closed his eyes. Uno sensed a deep loneliness. He decided to hang out with Chilly for a while.

Uno just sat there and watched Chilly for the next ten minutes. He seemed to be meditating. His eyes were closed, and his head hung low. He snored lightly for a minute, then snorted and woke up. He gazed around his surroundings slowly and then noticed Uno, quietly sitting up straight, still smiling at him. He chuckled.

"Come on, boy, how about a little walk? My back is getting stiff. Would you like to walk around the square with me?"

Uno let out a short, crisp bark.

"Yes, you are smart. Come on, Uno."

Chilly and Uno walked side by side, Uno looking up at him as he occasionally wavered with a slight limp. They walked past Mr. Haggeman's furniture store, and Chilly wobbled as they approached the sturdy, age-old Union National Bank, but caught his balance. A battered pickup truck backfired as they entered the town square, and Chilly froze for a moment, a painful look on his face.

The Macomb square was a grand old Midwestern town center. It was the community's beating heart, witness to a multitude of events, parades, and family outings since the 1830s when Macomb hit the map. A bustling burg in the center of the state, forty miles east of the Iowa border, Macomb was the seat of McDonough County. It took its name from General Alexander Macomb, a hero of the War of 1812. One of the town's claims to fame was a "Lincoln visit." In August 1858, U.S. senatorial candidate Abraham Lincoln denounced slavery in a speech to a sizable crowd in Macomb. A newspaper article described Honest Abe's oratorical style as a "conversation with friends."

In the center of the town square sat the majestic county courthouse, towering proudly over the ever-changing stores and shops encircling the square. Macomb boasted a population of 19,000 in 1976 and was the home of Western Illinois University, founded as a teacher's college at the turn of the 20th century. It was the hub of commercial and social activity for residents of thirty-three small towns in the county spanning a 70-mile radius.

As they turned the corner toward Ring's department store, a young boy whizzed by on a bicycle and shouted, "Hey Chilly, buy me a beer!" Uno looked up and saw Chilly turn his head away, ignoring the insulting remark. Uno could sense Chilly's hurt and saw images flash across Chilly's mind—snapshots of people hurling rude and derogatory comments at him as he walked around town. Uno was familiar with this type of ridicule. Back in the day, they called the recipients of this kind of mockery village idiots or town drunks. Disabled people, mentally challenged souls, alcoholics, and drug addicts—Uno had always embraced them with compassion. They, like all beings, were loved and supported beyond measure by a Universal Creative Intelligence that religions refer to as their God.

Chilly certainly wasn't an idiot. He graduated at the top of his Macomb High School Class of 1935, excelling in mathematics. His family had no money to send him to college, so he worked at the local iron foundry for several years after high school until he eagerly joined the Marines after the Japanese attacked Pearl Harbor. He earned three Purple Hearts during his service at Guadalcanal and the Solomon and Marshall Islands and witnessed horrors no human being could or should ever imagine.

Chilly was still cursed with nightmares of those atrocities 34 years later. After the war, he returned to work at the foundry until it closed its doors in 1968. He retired with a modest pension at age 55 and cozied up to the bottle. For the most part, he was content. He had several friends at the V.F.W., and the only real negatives in his life were the vicious hangovers, occasional hurtful taunts, and hellish nightmares, which had become less frequent as he aged.

Uno felt embarrassed when several people shouted, "Hi, Uno!" as they passed by. "They should be greeting Chilly with the same kindness," he thought.

Chilly and Uno took a right turn at Scott's Pharmacy on the northwest corner of the square and walked another block, returning to the same park bench in Chandler Park. The sun was high overhead now, warming everything in its sight. Chilly leaned back and took another pull from his bottle. He gave Uno another glance, smiled, and closed his eyes. Uno moved closer, laying his head on Chilly's thigh. Without opening his eyes, Chilly placed his hand on Uno's back.

Uno could still sense Chilly's pain. At that moment, Uno felt such love for this man. He focused all his energy on Chilly and began to pray.

"I know for Chilly that he is whole, perfect, and complete, exactly as he is. He lacks absolutely nothing to be the perfect soul that he is. I know for him that he releases any false and limiting beliefs that he is 'less than,' broken, defective, or anything other than perfect and blessed. He knows that people who think of him as lacking in any way, do not know his truth, but he and God do. He turns his thoughts toward that Loving Inner Presence whenever another being attempts to hurt or ridicule him, knowing that nothing can alter his true spiritual nature. He forgives others easily, and he forgives himself for perceiving a false reality. Through this forgiveness, Chilly maintains the peace, self-love, and love for others that is his birthright. I know for Chilly that he easily talks about the evils in the world he has witnessed with whoever is willing to listen, and the power of his harsh memories fades from his mind as he does so. I know for Chilly that he faces all mental challenges head on and sees their fallacy. He does not deny or fear any dark thought or feeling he has. He looks them square in the face, rejects their realism, and then speaks the truth to himself—that he is loved and loving, at peace within himself, and grateful for the life he has. I know for Chilly that he continually looks for opportunities to make himself and others happy. He serves his earthly brothers and sisters, and himself. He is grateful for and sure of his intimate relationship with God. I know this to be the truth about Chilly and give thanks for this truth coursing through me. I know my word manifests into a new reality for Chilly, right here, right now."

As Uno dozed off into a deep sleep, his mind bonded with Chilly's and they both dreamed of a warm embrace enveloping them in unconditional love and an indescribable peace.

Here are a few **truth affirmations** and random thoughts related
to *releasing the past, disregarding the false, loving ourselves,
and knowing our own truth.* They are written in the first-person
voice just for you and are "Uno-approved."

- I know who I am today. I am confident of my identity as a perfect spiritual being.
- I am a perfect creation of a Perfect Creator.
- I let go of any thought or belief that I am not enough. I know I am more than enough.
- I let go of the backward-looking past as I happily move forward.
- I speak only truth to myself.
- I accept the peace that is already mine, and I turn my mind away from false and limiting thoughts and beliefs.
- Other people may try to tell me who I am, but I know better. I listen to the Voice of Love within that tells me I am whole, perfect, and complete exactly as I am.
- I forgive myself for thinking I was not enough. I know better now.
- I know who and whose I am.
- I surround myself with people who uplift and support me.
- I release the past and have an enthusiastic zest for my life.
- My past does not define me. I let it go and know I am perfect as I am today.
- God is showing me my inner light and using it for the betterment of the world.
- I let go of the past and hold onto the lessons I have learned.
- I love myself so much that I know when others do not speak my truth.
- I listen within for the truth and know that the truth is based in love.
- My past has made me stronger. My inner light shines like a glow stick that's been shaken up.
- I see others as good, like me, and I know they are doing their best.
- As I lose the past, I find myself . . . growing stronger.

- I ignore the inner voices that tell me I am not enough or less than. I love and respect myself.
- I forgive myself for thinking the past is still my reality.
- I accept new and healthy experiences in my life with a grateful heart.
- I am sure of who I am, a perfect spiritual creation. My certainty is like a rock.
- I associate with people who know the real me.
- The voice of insecurity may sometimes be loud, but it is weak. My strength is found in stillness.
- I drop the past from my mind and rise higher.
- I am strong enough to hear the negative voices for what they are, and I revel in my awesomeness.
- I let go of any desire to find happiness and peace outside myself. My inner light is shining brightly with love.
- My human personality is not who I am. I am so much more.
- I am so much more than what others see.
- I let go, I love.
- I see beauty in everything and everyone.
- I release and let go of the past chapters of my life, and I write new chapters using a pen made of love and peace.
- My past is only a set of memories fired up by brain cells. My reality is the life I create today.
- I breathe in, I breathe out, I move on.
- I let go of the past knowing there is nothing new there to see. I embrace the perfect present as I seek wisdom and peace within.
- I am not my past, I am the love that is within and all around me.
- God is love, I am made of God, I am made of love.
- My soul is made of love, I embody love, and I express love to everyone in my life.
- I am willing to talk about the painful past, so I can finally let it go.
- I shake off the past like a bird shaking water from its wings. I fly higher.
- When I let go, I grow.

- I do not need to add anything to myself to grow. I am already complete. I let go of the past, it no longer serves me.
- I let go of the past. I am free to grow and move forward.
- I am grateful for knowing who I am today and give thanks for continuous joy and peace.

Rhyming Affirmations

The past cannot change, I let it go,
I feel the love within and lean into its flow.

I know who I am, and I say it to myself,
I live in the now and put the past on a shelf.

I'm a spiritual being, that's who I be,
Love is my guide, most definitely.

I watch my thoughts and release those that are misleading,
God's love, within me, that's all I'm needing.

I forgive, I let go, I go with the flow,
I plant seeds of love and watch them grow.

I'm not inferior or broken, I know the real me,
I'm perfect as I am, the truth sets me free.

When an inner voice tells me that I'm not enough,
I ignore it, I know better, I don't need to rebuff.

I drop the past, it has no power in the now,
Thoughts based in love are all that I allow.

I disregard the voices that I know speak fabrications,
and speak my truth with these awesome affirmations.

I surround myself with people who love and support,
and avoid the others like I would traffic court.

Uno's Random Thoughts

The problems we experience daily are grounded in our hidden core beliefs, which are formed at a young age. Most of us could benefit by talking to a therapist, spiritual practitioner, or minister to explore these core beliefs. We are spiritually and psychologically sick in varying forms. Yes, we are perfect at our core, but our human personalities are not. Talking aloud about our core beliefs and childhood experiences with someone who can guide us to the truth of ourselves can be a blessing beyond measure and a valuable growth experience.

Using the past to help us navigate the future is like using a rearview mirror to drive a car. The subconscious mind uses memories of the past to help us make sense of the world, but we can't rely solely upon what we already believe and think we know to move forward and grow. We must always be open to new ways of thinking and seeing the world. When something or someone is troubling us, the wisest thing we can say is, "How can I see this differently?"

A wise person has a mind that's like a blank screen, with few beliefs to filter incoming information. Openness, honesty, and a gentle self-discipline govern their mind. The wise person says, "Lead me, guide me, show me the way." When they say this, they are talking to that Perfect Presence within their mind—the one that answers every question and solves every problem.

If you've experienced trauma in your childhood—physical abuse, sexual abuse, verbal abuse—talk to someone about it. You need to expose it to the bright sunlight of truth. The way to do this is to talk about it with someone who can help you make sense of it. Painful experiences you've had as an adult can be obstacles, too—any type of violence, divorce, betrayal, sudden loss of a loved one, life upheavals, or any kind of trauma. You need to talk about it with someone! It doesn't matter how old you are. If you want less pain and more growth, get help.

Chapter 6
People Pleasing Performer

It was late fall, 1976, and the holidays were upon Uno and Deb. Thanksgiving was an incredible day in their home. Deb invited four of her single girlfriends over and prepared a feast beyond imagination. In truth, Deb didn't do all the cooking—they all pitched in. Deb's three-story, 80-year-old home was overflowing with positive energy. She and her friends hung out in the kitchen most of the day gossiping, laughing, and listening to swing and big band tunes on the radio. Turkey, ham, mashed potatoes, sweet potatoes, stuffing, green bean casserole, hot rolls, and cranberry sauce—the house smelled appetizing. Uno was right there in the kitchen, witnessing it all, moving from one friend to another, begging for scraps. By the time dinner was ready in the late afternoon, he was already full—what a day.

Then Deb dropped the bombshell—she was leaving for a one-week vacation to her favorite tropical paradise, the island of Kauai. Uno had visions of being jailed in a dog kennel or left alone in the house; but of course, Deb would never do that to her boy. He heard her on the phone, asking a friend to take him in for the week.

When Deb delivered Uno to Lori's home, Deb cried as she said goodbye. Uno shed a tear as well. Not a day had gone by since last

May that he hadn't slept with Deb and cuddled with her every morning as she awoke.

Lori was like an angel, so loving and attentive. Her husband Greg was good-natured as well, always laughing. Both in their forties, they lived in a spacious one-story modern home in the Meadowbrook subdivision on the outskirts of Macomb. The best part of this week-long experience was Janiece, their 16-year-old daughter. She was cute as could be—short blonde hair, light blue eyes, and a smile that made the grumpiest people feel good.

Janiece was excited to have a new friend for a week. Being an only child, she needed the company. Lori and Greg were attentive, caring parents, but nothing could compare to the love of a dog. But Janiece wasn't completely alone in her bedroom every night. She owned a cat named Sprinkles. When Uno arrived, Lori feared that Uno and Sprinkles would clash and "send the fur flying."

Sprinkles was unpredictable. She was lying in her usual spot on the end of a long, cream-colored sofa when Uno entered the house. Lori removed Uno's leash, and there was silence in the home as all three stood and watched. Uno slowly approached Sprinkles as she lay on the couch. Sprinkles sat up quickly, eyeing the stranger. Uno stopped, sat down, and with all the mental energy he could muster, launched a series of thoughts at Sprinkles.

"Hello, my name is Uno. I'll be living here, but only for a few days. I know you and I will be good friends. I adore cats. Your species are the gods and goddesses of the animal kingdom. I promise to be kind and loving to you and your family, and I recognize that you're the queen of this home. Will you allow me to stay?"

Sprinkles just stared at Uno, blinking twice. Silence in her mind.

"I don't think her receiver is working," thought Uno. "But it's clear she understood me in some way, perhaps on an emotional level. I sense a definite calmness."

Uno took a step closer to Sprinkles, and Sprinkles responded, inching closer toward the edge of the sofa cushion. They touched noses. Everyone in the room gasped, holding their breath. Uno gave Sprinkles a lick, and she closed her eyes, allowing him to give her five more licks before she sat up and gazed at Uno, then at Lori, Greg, and Janiece. Sprinkles turned around, curled up in a ball, and continued her catnap.

"Wow, did you see that?" whispered Lori. "I have never seen a dog and cat react to each other like that. Not on their first encounter, anyway."

Greg held his hand to his forehead in disbelief. "Me neither. Sprinkles has never responded that way to a dog. Remember that meeting with Goliath, the Great Dane your friend Paula owns?"

"Yeah, that time with Goliath was a rush," giggled Janiece. "I've never heard Sprinkles hiss so loudly."

Lori walked into the kitchen. "I think this dog is special. Come on, Uno, I bought you some Alpo. Are you hungry?"

Uno thought, "Am I hungry? Are fire hydrants red?"

After chowing down, Uno explored the house. It smelled like cat. Sprinkle's scent was everywhere, especially at the end of Janiece's bed.

"Fine," thought Uno. "Sprinkles can have Janiece's feet and I'll take her head." The thought of sleeping alone made Uno feel uneasy.

"Mom, can we take Uno with us today to the nursing home?"

"I don't see why not. I'm sure all those seniors would love to meet Uno, and I don't want to leave him all alone on his first day."

Today was a special day for Janiece. She was performing with her high school swing choir at The Elms nursing home. The MHS Swing Choir had a reputation for excellence. It was led by Mrs. Ruth Parks, an icon at Macomb High. In her fifties, she had taught music at the high school for over 20 years, and all the kids loved her. She was upbeat, energetic, and loved music. Every nursing home administrator in Macomb knew her because she firmly believed that young people, music, and senior citizens were a captivating mixture. The kids loved performing to the grateful seniors, and the seniors adored all that music and positive energy. Mrs. Parks was a gifted matchmaker.

The activity room at The Elms was full. It was a sizable forty by forty foot room, and Mr. Vick, the activities director at The Elms, had cleared space for the small 3-piece ensemble of piano, bass, and drums, with plenty of space in front of the crowd for the song and dance group to cut loose.

Uno sat on the floor in front of Lori. He was filled with excitement, taking in all the sights and sounds. Mrs. Anstine, a 75-year-old retired teacher sitting next to Lori, couldn't keep her hands off of Uno. Suddenly, the music started.

The drummer tapped out a quick and steady beat on the drum kit's muted hi-hat cymbals. Sixteen teenagers in attractive red, blue, and gold costumes ran into the activities room to the beat of the cymbals and took their positions in front of the crowd. The piano music filled the room with a cheerful, uplifting tune, and the kids sang with stunning energy.

"Oh, when the saints, go marching in! Oh, when the saints go marching in!"

Uno looked around at the audience. The seniors were giddy, letting all that divine music wash over them—the smiles, the joy, the magnificent sounds offered up to the crowd with such energy. Song after song, the kids shuffled, skipped, sashayed, stomped, and raised and lowered their arms with joy, smiling those giant smiles. Uno had never seen two groups of people so happy—the kids singing and dancing, and the seniors, wholly absorbed in the performance.

Toward the end of the group's final song, Uno couldn't take it any longer. He broke free of Lori and bolted toward the kids. He weaved in and out of the dancing legs until he found Janiece and raised on his hind legs, reaching for her. Janiece was both shocked and thrilled, laughing hysterically. The other kids kept dancing around Uno while the audience laughed loudly and pointed. Janiece reached down and quickly lifted Uno into her arms, continuing the dance routine. Uno was now part of the choir as Janiece held him tightly, singing, dancing, and laughing simultaneously. The group positioned themselves for the song's finale, raising their arms into the air and striking their song-ending pose. On the last note, Uno howled like a frisky wolf to put a punctuation mark on the performance. The entire room roared with applause and laughter, as the seniors happily struggled to rise from their chairs and give the group a standing ovation.

Janiece and her parents talked about Uno's surprise performance later over dinner. He was the star of the show today, even though that wasn't his intention. Uno simply couldn't contain his unbridled joy and *had* to be part of the performance. Later in the evening, while lying on Janiece's bed, he thought again about his life purpose and saw a parallel—he *had* to be a part of this world right now.

But all was not roses, love poems, and unicorns in Janiece's mind. Uno was disturbed when both he and Janiece quieted their thoughts and were drifting off to sleep. There was a murkiness permeating her consciousness. Uno was somehow sure that her parents were not aware of it. As Uno surveyed her deepest thoughts and beliefs, he sensed a mental cloudiness in her subconscious mind. Uno concentrated harder.

"Aha!" thought Uno. "There it is." Janiece craved the approval of others. In the past, Uno heard this referred to as a need for approval. He knew it was not a need, but a desire. Approval from others is like a patch covering a hole in someone's psyche. The hole is the hidden core belief of "I am not enough."

In Janiece's case, this belief formed early in life. It started when she was told she needed to be a "good girl." Her parents expected much from her but gave her little recognition or positive reinforcement. They told her she was "special" and "gifted," but didn't routinely praise her achievements. Lori and Greg expected A's, and Janiece earned them. They expected her to show her talents, and she did. But their acknowledgments were never enough for Janiece. They did not overly criticize her, but neither did they simply accept and love her for who she was, flaws and all. People pleasing begins with parent pleasing.

Janiece's desire for approval manifested itself in all her relationships—with her friends, teachers, her Lutheran minister, and especially with herself. She wanted approval of her looks and body, her personality, and her skills, talents, and goals. She was never "good enough" for her harshest critic, herself.

Uno knew that these false and limiting core beliefs she held overshadowed any relationship she had with her True Self. She did not fully grasp her true spiritual nature as a divine being, a reflection of God. When someone is confident of their true mystical identity, they love themselves unconditionally and listen within for guidance and recognition. Their God-Self praises them. They sustain a positive and nurturing relationship with themselves and have little desire for outside approval. They are content.

Uno knew what he needed to affirm for Janiece. As he planted these divine creative seeds into the One Universal Mind, he also knew she would accept and embody them. Uno curled up closely to Janiece's head as she slept. He nuzzled his snout into her sweet-smelling hair and prayed.

"I know for Janiece that she is immaculate and exquisite precisely as she is. Her soul is a reflection of God's essence—perfection. At her core, she is a finished product, needing nothing to be the purely eminent soul she already is. She shares the same God qualities as the Infinite Loving Consciousness that continually creates all life. I know for Janiece that she recognizes false and limiting beliefs for what they are, misperceptions of truth—flawed images. She acknowledges these beliefs and releases them from her consciousness. When and if they surface in her conscious mind, she denies them her attention.

Janiece is confident of the knowledge of her true nature—whole, perfect, and complete. I know for her that she knows, beyond all doubt, that she is more than enough. Her True Self confidently reinforces this knowledge through her inner dialogue. An Inner Light continually praises her, uplifts her, supports her, and guides her. She tunes into this Powerful Inner Presence through prayer, personal affirmation, mindfulness, and silence. She listens, she accepts, and she loves herself deeply. These words faithfully describe Janiece's truth. Period. I give thanks for it and simply release it into the Divine One Mind, which echoes back this truth into her consciousness and life. Thank you, Sacred Love."

Here are a few **truth affirmations** and random thoughts related to *releasing the desire for approval (people pleasing), self-love, and knowing our own truth.* They are written in the first-person voice just for you and are "Uno-approved."

- I am living to please myself, not others. I am content when I am aligned with my values.
- I know my truth; others may think they do.
- I trust myself to think, feel, and act in alignment with God.
- My ideas, thoughts, and feelings matter because they are mine.
- My happiness is not connected to other people. I am happy because I'm secure in myself and love myself.
- I release any desire to please others to win their approval. I am content within myself.
- I let go of any fear related to displeasing others. I am true to myself and fulfilled by living in alignment with my values.
- I love others, and I also have boundaries. I let others be who they are, and I am content with myself.
- I let go of any belief that tells me I am responsible for how others feel.
- I am a spiritual being. I know I am one with others. I am a human being, I have boundaries.
- I say "yes" to myself and release the perceived need to continually say it to others.
- I know that what others think of me is none of my concern.
- I release any desire to impress others, I simply love them.
- I honor and respect myself by telling myself the truth, always.
- I deserve all good things in life.
- God loves me, I feel it within. God's love is enough.
- I can love people from afar. I can pray for them, I can forgive them, and I can say "no" to them.

- Regardless of how this turns out, I am okay. I am always okay.
- I know who loves me regardless of what I think, feel, say, or do. God loves me, and I love myself.
- I let go of others' opinions of me.
- I always do what's best for me.
- My happiness and self-worth are up to me.
- I lovingly accept responsibility for my peace of mind.
- I love my life, and my life loves me back.
- I let go of any desire to defend myself.
- I live and love with integrity, and I'm happy with myself.
- I release all doubts and insecurities about myself.
- I deserve and accept the love that I also give to others.
- I am a masterpiece, and I have mastered peace.
- I am open and willing to become the next best version of myself.
- I let go of all comparisons. I love myself the way I am.
- I am not less than, I am not better than, I am content with who I am.
- As I love myself more, my life gets better and better.
- I forgive myself for any mistakes I think I've made, and I love myself.
- I am an inspiration to myself.
- God made only one of me. I am unique, blessed, and grateful.
- I go within and imagine the best version of myself. This is who I really am.
- I love myself more and more each minute.
- I value myself, and I value my values.
- I let go of any desire to be understood by others. I understand myself, and that's enough.
- I let go of everything that weighs me down, and I rise higher.
- No one does life quite like me.
- I'm not just worthy of love and joy, I AM love and joy.

- Dear Self, I love you!
- I live life on my own terms. My terms are happiness, love, and inner peace.
- I turn away from any inner voice that criticizes me. I don't need to defend myself in my mind. I love myself.

Rhyming Affirmations

God loves me, I feel it within.
When I need love, I turn within again.

I love myself no matter what others think,
My self and my worth are entirely in sync.

I'm okay, and you're okay,
My life is as sweet as a flower bouquet.

I take others' opinions of me with a grain of salt,
Happy and loving are my new default.

I say "yes" to myself and feel the inner peace,
I'm special, I'm loved, I'm an impressive masterpiece.

I trust myself, and I know the real me,
I treat myself most lovingly.

When I am attacked, I just know life can be rough,
But I know the real me, I know I'm enough.

I love myself, but I'm not conceited,
I'm a child of God—whole, perfect, and completed.

The best version of myself, that what I see,
it matters not at all if you disagree.

I let go of self-criticism, and I rise higher,
I do this often, I'm a frequent flyer.

Uno's Random Thoughts

People pleasing often starts with parent pleasing. Winning mom and dad's approval by being a good girl or boy is at the heart of inner insecurities. Let mom and dad go! Be content with yourself! You can be madly in love with yourself and not be arrogant or self-centered. Self-love is grounded in the knowledge that you are a perfect spiritual being. "Perfect" means you lack nothing, and you are perfect as you are, like a beautiful rose. A rose may have a blemish, but it's still perfect as it is.

With more self-understanding comes the awareness that we hurt ourselves more than anyone hurts us. As we realize that our self-limiting, self-critical thoughts and beliefs are just a fabrication and nothing more, we can easily let them go. Being watchful of our thoughts is the key. But don't criticize your critical thoughts because that just adds more criticism. Just be aware of them. The more we are aware, the more we are in the present moment, the home of inner peace.

Be kind and gentle with yourself. If someone criticizes or judges you, ask yourself if there's any truth to what they're saying. If there is, make a correction and move on. Forgive yourself for being human and forgive others for judging you. Just know that your happiness is not dependent on others. Generate joy from within. You are a creative being, made in the image of a Universal Creator, however you define the Infinite. Use your creative power to create the self you want to be.

Chapter 7
Good Grief, Uno

"Oh no, Deb is crying! What's wrong?!" Uno jumped up on the bed with Deb and snuggled up close to her face, giving it several energetic licks.

"Oh, Uno, I love you so much," said Deb between sobs.

Uno didn't understand. He just knew his stepmom was crying, and her pain was deep and overwhelming. He nuzzled his snout into her neck, whimpering. Deb squeezed Uno tightly. He lay with her for several more minutes until the silence was interrupted by the sound of her deep breathing. She had fallen asleep.

Uno gently freed himself from Deb's arms and stealthily wriggled off the bed. He scurried down the creaking wooden stairs and began looking for clues related to Deb's anguish. He crept through the kitchen, dining room, and living room, looking for any indicators.

Uno jumped on the couch and inspected the coffee table in front of it. "There it is," he thought. "It's a telegram." He straddled the coffee table and began reading.

"I sincerely apologize for making this notification by telegram, but we haven't been able to reach you by phone."

"Yep, this is it. Deb's phone has been out of service for the last few days." He continued reading.

"Your mother passed peacefully in her sleep on the evening of the 12th. Her body is in stasis at the Harrison County Medical Examiner's Office as we await further instructions from you. Please accept our deepest condolences. Your mother will be dearly missed here at the Autumn Winds Nursing Home."

Uno felt so sad for Deb. He knew she loved her mother, Maxine, very much. Two years earlier, Maxine's dementia had progressed to the point of institutionalization, and the Autumn Winds in tiny Gladstone, Illinois, was the only care facility within a 50-mile radius that Deb and her brother could afford. Deb and Tim visited Maxine weekly, either together or separately, but had missed a week because of the holidays. Uno was heartbroken that Deb learned of her mother's passing this way.

The next few weeks were rough for Deb. She had many details to handle—the cremation, death certificate, her mom's will and bank account, the obituary, arranging her mom's memorial service, and collecting her remaining possessions in Gladstone. "It was cruel," Uno thought, "that she had to work so hard to close out her mom's final chapter of life when she missed her so much." Tim tried to help, but he was a mess. He was a mama's boy, both he and Deb knew it.

Frank and Maxine Giddins were both in their late twenties when they relocated to Macomb in 1921. After serving in The Great War, Frank earned his master's degree in English and Literature at New York University, and his first teaching post was the newly re-named Western Illinois State Teachers College in West Central Illinois.

Twenty-eight-year-old Maxine was disappointed to relinquish her dream of becoming a Broadway star. Since 1913, she'd played small speaking parts in several off-Broadway stage productions. Maxine loved the stage. But she loved Frank even more and was excited and eager to become a mother. Parenthood came rather quickly. Their son, Timothy Francis Giddins, was born in Macomb in 1923, and Deborah Lee arrived two years later.

By the time Deb graduated from Macomb High, World War II had siphoned off most of the young male workforce, and Maxine returned to work as a college secretary. By the late '40s, she was garnering lead roles in local productions and large-scale WIU stage shows. Maxine continued acting throughout the '50s and '60s while working her way up the administration ladder at WIU. Frank had a fatal coronary at the young age of 67 in 1960, and tireless Maxine continued working until she turned 70 in 1963. She was well-known and loved in this wholesome town of 19,000 souls, and her memorial service in early 1977 at the Immanuel Lutheran Church was jam-packed. Deb was mentally and emotionally exhausted by the time Maxine's ashes were laid in the ground.

Deb was a counselor assigned to McDonough District Hospital's Community Mental Health Center in Macomb. After twenty-six years as a counselor, she knew the signs and symptoms of oncoming depression like the back of her hand. She experienced a bout of depression ten years earlier when her ex-husband, Monte, an attorney, left Deb for his 23 year-old paralegal. The homewrecker's name was Fran, but everyone called her Frankie. Deb and her girlfriends nicknamed her, "Skanky Frankie."

Deb finally admitted to herself that she needed help. She spoke to Jonathan Rush, one of her colleagues at the mental health center, and he begged her to join his grief support group. Deb finally caved.

The Wednesday night grief support group was currently rather small with only eight folks, including Deb. Jonathan was a kind, compassionate, soft-spoken counselor and group leader. He was in his mid-thirties, tall, and prematurely gray, sporting a silver bushel of hair and a diamond stud in his left ear, which was a touch radical for 1977. His beautiful wife, Janelle, was a nurse at the hospital, and they had two toddlers at home, which might have explained his gray hair.

Deb decided to bring Uno with her to the weekly meetings. He was well behaved, and she didn't like leaving him alone at night since she worked all day. But those weren't the only reasons she decided to include him. Deb knew there was something unique about Uno. She had never known or heard of a dog who related to people as he did.

The group sat in comfortable padded chairs in a circle, and Uno sat next to Deb on the floor. But he didn't lie down, as other dogs might. He sat straight up and looked from person-to-person as each of them talked, as if he understood what they were saying—it looked spooky unless you knew Uno.

When someone cried, Uno left Deb's side, approached the crying person, and put his two front paws on their knees, as if to say, "I'm here for you." The group was amazed and amused whenever he did this, and the person crying would inevitably either laugh or cry harder.

People heal as they talk, and the grief support group allowed folks to talk about their feelings openly. As a counselor, Deb did very little grief counseling over the years. Now she was the counselee and was open to healing. Grief is individual and personal. Each person experiences it differently, and the coping mechanisms that people use are driven by their personality. Some people walk through grief within a few weeks; for others, it could take years. The common denominator in healing one's mind, Deb learned, was the experience of talking about your grief, and the insights gained by actually verbalizing your feelings aloud to other humans. The folks who "hurt" the most were those who clammed up. They could be in pain for years.

As the weeks rolled on, Deb's grief lessened slightly. Other group members experienced similar relief. She began to see patterns in their emotional reactions. Like Deb, two other group members lost someone within the last few weeks. They experienced shock, disbelief, and an intense sadness whenever they thought of their loved one. Jonathan said these feelings were normal, and without talking about one's sadness, people feel a sense of isolation. Silent grievers think no one can understand their grief, which deepens the sorrow even more. For Deb, it was the little reminders of her mother that tweaked her heartache—the scent of her mom's perfume, a favorite food, or a reminder of a memory. She still cried when she thought, "Oh, wow, I should tell mom about this or that," and then remembered mom was gone. But this happened less and less as time passed.

One of the group members, Sharon, was still entrenched in guilt. Three months earlier, this 45 year-old woman, who cared for her disabled mother in her home, left her car running in the garage and mindlessly closed the garage door as she always did. Then Sharon went for a long walk, stopping at the Ford Hopkins drug store soda fountain for a cherry coke. When she returned home, her mother was dead, asphyxiated from carbon monoxide. Sharon attempted suicide and was institutionalized for a month. Thankfully, the district attorney, like many other people in Macomb, felt compassion for her. Sharon's guilt complicated her grief because, like Deb, she loved and missed her mom so much. Deb predicted that Sharon would be in therapy for at least a year, maybe longer. Uno always jumped up in Sharon's lap whenever she wept. Sharon would hug him tightly as she talked.

Thirty-year-old Jerry was angry. His wife of five years, Gracie, received a diagnosis for an incurable blood disease. The couple had no health insurance and little money. Gracie shot herself after leaving him a long letter expressing her love and defending her decision to commit suicide. Jerry was a quiet, logical type of person, but was hung up in anger. Six months had passed since Gracie's death and Jerry was still pissed at her. He blamed God, he blamed the hospital, but mostly he blamed Gracie for not allowing him to care for her. With Jonathan's help, Jerry was beginning to realize that her decision had nothing to do with him; it was her decision. More than that, Jerry was finally starting to talk about forgiveness. He was still holding on to some anger, though, thinking that it served him. Again, different coping mechanisms.

Fear paralyzed Sandy, who said she felt like she was hip deep in quicksand. She was 50 years old, had never worked, and her husband of 30 years, Gary, died in a one-car accident. No insurance money, no job, no skills, and she was obese, making it unlikely she would re-marry (her words). She was terrified of her financial future while trying to accept the loss of her best friend.

The most heartbreaking story in the group was Cheryl. This 43-year-old secretary at a law firm lost her husband to cancer six years ago. She still had an intense longing for him. She thought of him often, to the point of the thoughts becoming intrusive. She fantasized about her husband being alive and sometimes thought she saw him in a crowd. She still thought of her life as meaningless without him. Deb thought that Cheryl needed therapy, but Cheryl was afraid to let go of her fantasy world. She was another favorite for Uno. He would sometimes sit next to her and lean his head on her thigh, even when she wasn't talking.

Deb's grief support group had no idea how much Uno prayed for them. Every Wednesday night after the meeting, as Deb and Uno lay in bed, Uno affirmatively prayed for their grieving friends. The length and intensity of his prayers varied, depending on what he'd heard that evening in the meeting. But there were always common threads—releasing, letting go, forgiving, accepting "what is," healing, and loving one's self. Uno prayed for Deb too. He prayed for her every night as he lay down in bed, and every morning as she awoke, and he cuddled with her.

Four months after Deb's mom transitioned into the next expression of life, Uno saw her. The soul formerly known as Maxine visited Deb. It was her heavenly birthday (as Deb called it), and Deb cried several times that day. As Uno and Deb lay in bed, Uno was praying. He sensed a presence and looked up. There, hovering over Deb was a spirit. It didn't have a shape or human features; it was just a presence, Maxine's presence. Uno didn't know how he knew; he just did. Maxine's energy hovered over Deb and Uno could hear Maxine.

"I love you, my precious baby. I love you so much. I'm well. I'm loved. I'm at peace. I'm with others who guide me, and they are with you too. It's okay to let go, baby. It's okay. I will always love you, and we will be together again. I love you, sweetheart."

Then Uno felt Maxine hovering over him.

"Take care of my baby, Uno. I know you will. Thank you for knowing her truth for her. I love you, sweet doggy man."

Poof! Maxine was gone. Uno felt intense love and a profound calmness. The feeling was so familiar to him. He mentally centered himself and prayed for Deb.

"I know for Deb that she continues to experience and embody an overwhelming feeling of love in her mind, body, and soul. I know that this love results in a daily experience of peace, calmness, contentment, and a simple acceptance of life "as it is." Deb lets go of any dark or non-loving thoughts or feelings she has in connection with her mother. She feels only love for her mom and knows that her mother loves her. I know for Deb that she releases, she lets go, and does this in her own time, in her own way, and is graced by more love as she does so. I know this to be Deb's truth. I thank the universe and Maxine for helping me express this truth, and I plant it into the unformed substance to grow and thrive in the One Mind that my sweet Deb shares. And, so it is."

Here are a few **truth affirmations and messages to the Great Beyond** related to *dealing with grief, loving and communicating with people and furry friends who have passed, and loving ourselves as we grieve*. Affirmations are written in the first-person voice just for you and are "Uno-approved."

Messages to the Great Beyond

In case you're not sure what to say to people and furry friends who have passed.

- My eyes still look for you, my mind still thinks of you, and my heart knows you are happy and at peace.
- You will always be a part of me, and I'm so grateful for the time we had together.
- The love we shared embraces the pain I feel and makes it okay for now.
- The memories of you knock me down some days, but the love we shared picks me up and embraces me.
- I know there is no loss, you will always be with me.
- I know I am not alone. You and God are with me.

- I am grateful for everything you taught me, everything you gave me, and especially for the love we shared.
- I think of you often, and I know these mental reminders are your love flowing to me.
- I am holding onto our love and letting go of the idea of loss.
- I know that physical death is just a journey home and that the love and connection we have is forever.
- I know that the pain I feel is an expression of our love.
- I am letting go and still loving you.
- The qualities I loved most about you are the building blocks of the new me.
- I know that the sadness I feel is like a road sign on my journey, and not a destination.
- People tell me you and I will be together again, but I know we are not apart.
- I no longer hear your voice, but I still listen to you talking to my heart.
- My tears are a prayer to God to keep you enveloped in love.
- Missing you is my new way of saying how much I love you.
- The light you brought into the world is still here in my heart.
- Our bodies come to an end, but our love never does.

Affirmations

I am strong today because I'm ready to let go of sadness.

I know death is merely stepping out of this physical world and into the spiritual dimension, my real home.

I know there's no rush or time limits for grieving. I feel what I feel, and I allow my new life to unfold.

I am not rushing my healing. I know this sadness has something to teach me.

I know there is no afterlife, just a different expression of life.

Fear of death is just a fear of the unknown, but in my heart, I remember a spiritual realm.

I know that death is not an end, but the beginning of a new life.

I am ready to let go of my sorrow, as I continue to embrace my love for ____________.

I choose love today, I choose to heal.

I don't avoid, resist, or judge my sadness. I know it's natural and an expression of love.

I am kind and gentle with myself as I heal.

I let go of any guilt that my mind tells me I should feel for being happy. The happiness and peace I feel after so much sadness is a reflection of the love we shared.

Immortality is a universal truth. Life goes on in countless forms.

I allow peace to fill my soul.

Love continues forever.

In my sadness, I love myself.

Love is immortal; Like life, it never truly dies.

I am strong, courageous, and kind to myself all at the same time.

This passing storm makes my roots even stronger.

I don't know how or when this sadness will end. I'm just taking one step at a time and loving myself.

I never knew how strong I was until I realized that loving myself and being strong are the same.

This sadness has come to pass, not to stay.

Either I will find a way to get through this, or I will make one.

Even though my sadness seems overpowering at times, I know I will get through this.

Chapter 8

Shame on No One

In 1965, Deb's brother Tim became a father. His son Jeff was 21 years old when he met Tim. Confused? Tim was.

Before Tim left for the Pacific to fight the Japanese in 1943, he got his fiancée Judy pregnant, but she didn't tell him. Judy broke off the engagement with a Dear John letter about the time Tim was engaged in the Battle of Vella Gulf while assigned to the USS Dunlap in the South Pacific.

Judy and Tim had been students at Western when Tim lost his draft deferment in late 1942. He joined the Navy rather than being drafted into the Army. When Judy broke off the engagement in 1943, she moved back to Chicago with her parents, who tried unsuccessfully to convince her to marry Tim. Judy wanted nothing to do with him. She planned to split with Tim before she got pregnant, and when he departed for the Pacific, she took the opportunity to escape her situation in Macomb. The baby, Jeffrey, was born the following year and never knew his father.

At age 21 in 1965, Jeff was attending Illinois State University in Bloomington, majoring in theology. His grandmother Frieda, who had helped raise him along with Judy in Chicago, decided to tell him about his father. Judy was not happy that her mother betrayed her trust but chose to handle the situation with honesty and openness. Mother and son had a heartfelt discussion, and she apologized to him for keeping his father's existence a secret. Jeff was shocked, confused, and angry. It took him several weeks to come to terms with the fact that he actually did have a father.

By the time he made contact with Tim in Macomb, he was excited and eager to meet the man he never knew existed. Tim was shocked, confused, and angry as well. But all those emotions and the ensuing drama gave way to acceptance, and finally happiness, that he had a son. But the joy he felt was clouded in fear and trepidation when he finally met Jeff.

That was 12 years ago. Jeff was now 34 years old and a Methodist minister in Springfield, about 80 miles southeast of Macomb. He visited his dad three or four times a year and had spent several holidays with Tim and his aunt Deb over the years. Jeff even convinced his mother, Judy, to join his father and aunt in Macomb for a Thanksgiving dinner back in 1970. That was an awkward day for Judy and Tim, but a day Jeff never forgot—his mother and father sitting at the same dinner table.

It was a gorgeous spring day in April 1977 when Jeff came to spend the weekend with his dad. Whenever he visited, Deb slept over at Tim's house too. As she liked to say, "Tim and Jeff can't cook worth a squat, and I need to look after my two men."

"Hey, it's Uno!" shouted Jeff as Deb and Uno walked in through Tim's back door.

Jeff sat on the living room floor, rubbing Django's belly. Uno leapt onto Jeff and smothered him with kisses. Django jumped to his feet and sprang on Jeff too. The three of them rolled around on the thick beige carpet, Jeff laughing hysterically.

Deb prepared BLTs for lunch. Jeff was animated as they ate, telling Tim and Deb the latest news of his church and some of the challenges his congregants were experiencing. Deb and Tim listened intently. They were so proud of Jeff. As an assistant pastor, he was such a positive influence on his church. He had created new spiritual programs, reinvigorated the dwindling Bible study group, and established a new home visit ministry. The senior pastor, Reverend Clyde, admired his new assistant and valued his youthful energy.

"Deb, can we talk privately?" murmured Jeff as he helped his aunt clear the table.

"Sure, let's go out on the patio."

"Tim honey, Jeff and I are going out to the patio," Deb whispered to Tim in the living room. "He said he needed to talk privately. I think I might need to put on my counselor hat."

"Sure, okay. There's a Charlie Chan movie on the tube today. I'll be right here."

Django flopped down next to Tim as he turned on the TV, and Uno decided to join Deb and Jeff in the back yard. As they sat down on the patio lawn chairs, Jeff began speaking to Deb, and he immediately choked up.

"What is it honey, what's wrong?"

"I was arrested yesterday, Deb. I feel so ashamed."

"Arrested? For what?"

"Well, not arrested, really. I was issued a citation, and I have to appear in court. I... uh... man, this is hard."

"It's okay, honey, you can tell me. You know I love you, and you can trust me." Deb always knew the right thing to say in those awkward moments.

"Well, I... uh... (pause)... I was cited for indecent exposure."

"Oh." Deb paused, leaned back in her chair, and gathered her thoughts. She hadn't expected this.

"It was at one of those... uh... peep shows. A place out on route 29, north of Springfield."

"Oh, I see. Where they show the girly movies."

"Right. I feel so ashamed. I uh.... exposed myself to an undercover police officer and was cited for indecent exposure. I have to appear in court next month. I don't know what's going to happen to my job, and I'm so afraid my citation will appear in the newspaper."

"Well, I would ask you how this makes you feel, but you've already told me twice. Ashamed."

"Yeah, and fear. I feel this knot in my gut, and I haven't been able to think of anything else."

"That's a normal reaction. Until you get some resolution regarding your job and Reverend Clyde, you're probably going to feel some fear. For now, there's nothing you can do about it, so you've got to let it go."

"Believe me, I've tried. The thoughts and feelings just won't stop."

"Let me ask you a question, Jeff. I know that your religious beliefs, your... uh... faith... is strong. Am I right?"

"Well yes, but..."

"But nothing. From what I know about the Bible, it says something like, 'God forgives all sins.' He forgives them without you even having to ask, right?"

"Right. That's pretty much what scripture says."

"Well then, if God forgives you, who are you not to forgive yourself?"

"Yeah, I hear what you're saying..."

"Let me ask you something else. Are you homosexual?"

Jeff started to speak and then stopped. There was a long pause as he looked off into the distance. He began to cry.

"Aunt Deb, no one has ever asked me that question."

"You don't need to answer it right now, or ever. I love you without any conditions. The reason I'm asking is to discover whether your sex life—your natural desires, your self-image—are causing you to feel shame. If so, I think you need to talk to someone besides me, a therapist who specializes in shame."

"I've never really thought about all this in depth."

"Jeff, let me tell you something. Shame is corrosive. It's toxic. It's an intense feeling or belief that we are somehow flawed or unworthy of love. The human ego wants to hide the shame and not talk about it, but the less we talk about shame, the more power it has over our minds. On the other hand, the more we talk about it, in a nonjudgmental environment with a trusted person, the less power it has to make us feel miserable and self-critical. The more we name it and see it for what it is, the quicker it evaporates."

Jeff began crying again. Uno instantly jumped on his lap and eagerly licked his face. Jeff laughed and hugged Uno tight.

Deb laughed too. "Do you see that love Uno is giving you? That's the same kind of love you'll be giving yourself after you get some help from a therapist. Accepting and loving yourself has nothing to do with your position as a minister. That's a separate topic, and I know you'll deal with your citation and your job openly and honestly, but therapy is important to your future well-being."

"I think you're right. I've been hiding for too long. I've never talked to anyone about this."

"That's what shame does. It keeps us silent."

Deb and Jeff continued talking for another hour. She helped Jeff put together a plan to find a therapist and to talk to Reverend Clyde first thing Monday morning. They ended their talk with a long, warm hug. The sun was setting as they went back into the house. The TV movie had finished, and Tim had his feet up on the ottoman, fast asleep.

Whenever Jeff visited his dad, Uno slept with Deb, as he always did. But tonight, Uno was waiting for Jeff in his bed. Jeff laughed.

"Are you sleeping with me tonight, buddy?" Uno raised his head and smiled at Jeff, walking to the foot of the bed and curling up in a ball.

Jeff's mind felt so much clearer as he drifted off to sleep. When Uno felt Jeff's breathing slow down, he knew he was asleep. Uno crept up the side of the bed next to Jeff and lay down next to him, placing his snout on Jeff's head. Uno closed his eyes and centered himself, opening his mind to Jeff.

Uno could feel the shame immediately. It felt like an overbearing, judgmental presence. Uno envisioned it as a big, ugly ogre, a monster. He saw flashes of images—Jeff having sex with men, Jeff drinking alone, Jeff in a Bible class looking uneasy. He felt judgment, self-loathing, self-criticism, disappointment, fear, a kind of hopelessness, and caught a glimpse of a dim suicidal thought. Jeff was in so much pain. Uno had to stop for a moment. He was feeling what Jeff was feeling, and it overwhelmed him.

Uno paused and then re-centered his mind, connecting to the One Divine Mind.

"I know for Jeff that he is perfect, just as he is. I know that he accepts this truth wholeheartedly. I know he lets go of any thoughts and beliefs that falsely tell him that he is flawed, broken, not enough, or separate or different from others. He is at peace with every decision he has made and every action he has taken. Jeff is wholly and holy innocent based on who he really is—a perfect creation of a Perfect Creator. I know for Jeff that he is as God originally made him—innocent, pure, loved, loving, happy and joyful, and at total peace with himself. He treats himself with loving kindness. He listens to that inner Loving Voice that tells him his truth, and he disregards other people or any inner voice that tells him lies about his identity and human nature. I know for Jeff that he accepts himself totally. He knows beyond all doubt that there's nothing wrong with him, and everything about him is right within God's eyes. I know for Jeff that he loves himself deeply and that this self-love is expressed in his thoughts and beliefs. Jeff's consciousness is overflowing with joy, peace, love, and a profound certainty of his genuine divine identity. He is centered, at peace, and grateful for knowing who and whose he is. Thank you for allowing this truth about Jeff to flow through me. I plant it into the universal unformed substance and gratefully watch it manifest in Jeff's life."

Here are a few **truth affirmations** and random thoughts related to *releasing shame and loving and accepting ourselves*. They are written in the first-person voice just for you and are "Uno-approved."

- I am innocent!
- I release all thoughts and beliefs related to shame. I am perfect as I am.
- I let go of all self-judgmental thoughts and simply love myself.
- I am at peace with my past. I pour all painful memories into a pool of love.
- I turn away from the critical voice within, and I choose love and joy.
- I let go of all that hurts.
- I deserve all the good that life has to offer.
- I am worthy of love from myself and others.
- I am amazingly amazing.
- I am coated with awesome sauce.
- My mind is stilled in serenity, and I hear the truth.
- I let go of the past and create the life I want.
- My mistakes activate and energize a loving and forgiving Presence within me, which guides my thinking.
- I am in complete control of my own happiness and peace of mind.
- I am doing my best, and that's more than enough.
- My possibilities are endless. My potential is infinite.
- Above all, I am kind and gentle with myself.
- I do not accept other people's judgment—shame and guilt are NOT who I am. I am a perfect creation of a Perfect Creator who teaches me daily how to love myself more.
- I believe in myself. I am my own cheerleader.
- Something wonderful is happening through me right now. It is love, and I accept and embody it.

- My human personality makes mistakes. At my core, I am a perfect spiritual being. I forgive myself for my human mistakes. I know they are not who I am. I love myself deeply.
- I am true to myself. My behavior is aligned with my spiritual values.
- I am an expression of harmony. I have perfect balance of body, mind, and spirit.
- I attract love into my life by loving myself.
- I let go of all judgments and critical thoughts of others and myself. I am peace in expression.
- I am flexible and forgiving, both with myself and others.
- I deserve to heal. I am worth it.
- I am worthy of all things wonderful and good.
- I summon my God-given powers of creativity to move my life forward in the most positive direction.
- I release any desire to change the past, and I love myself in the present moment.
- The storms of my past came to clear the way for me to love and respect myself.
- I am in total alignment with my life purpose.
- I inspire others.
- I honor the progress I have made, and I stand firmly with my values.
- I like where I am, and I am ready for new opportunities.
- I create the me that I want to be.
- I allow myself to be fully loved by God and my family and friends.
- I am choosing to follow love in all that I think, say, and do.
- God is bigger than any problem I think I have.
- I choose what I become.
- I have the power to change my story.
- I let go of all self-criticism. I am grateful for my mistakes and use them to move forward.

- I value genuine connection with others, not validation or approval.
- I am filled with love and compassion.
- I attract the love that I am.

Rhyming Affirmations

I am worthy of all the good that life has to give,
Self-worth and gratitude, that's how I live.

I am entirely ready for more opportunity,
I am immersed in life and loving the unity.

My mistakes don't define me, they're not who I am,
I love myself dearly, I never condemn.

I can't change the past, I let it go,
I focus on today and get in the flow.

I progress, I move forward, I learn, I grow,
I don't hope that I'm better. I feel it, I know.

"What would LOVE do?" I ask when I'm uncertain or in doubt,
Love is the solution, the healer; it's what life's all about.

I choose what I am. I take complete responsibility,
Total freedom, unlimited, and open to all possibility.

I turn my attention away from foolish self-criticism,
Self-love washes away the darkness and cynicism.

I don't need or want others' approval or validation,
An inner loving Presence is my rock, my foundation.

I'm overflowing with love for you and for me,
I'm grateful that I can love so passionately.

Uno's Random Thoughts

Shame is toxic. It's like a cancer of the psyche. Guilt says, "You've done something bad." Shame says, "You ARE bad." Everyone's consciousness is burdened with a certain amount of shame. Some people are weighed down with it, like toddlers trying to carry a 50-pound rock on their shoulders, and they don't even know it. We must rid ourselves of shame to be completely free and happy. We do this by exploring our past, our childhood, our experiences, and our core beliefs about ourselves. We explore with the help of a trusted professional, someone who can guide us in our self-understanding.

"I am not enough" is an evil belief. We intuitively know we don't want this belief, so we project it out onto others. It turns into, "You are not enough." Someone who is always angry at the world is filled with shame. They were taught to think negatively about themselves by people who thought negatively about themselves.

We will never be happy about what's "out there" until we learn to love ourselves.

With self-understanding comes self-love. The solution is within. The ego says, "No, look out there, not in here." The ego hates introspection, self-reflection, and especially quiet meditation. As powerful as the ego seems, it's not a separate self and has no Real power. "Real" with a capital "R" indicates something shares God's essence. *The ego is not Real.* It's merely a human-made collection of beliefs. The ego is NOT who you are. The Perfect Presence within you is Real. God within answers every question and solves every problem when asked to do so. You don't even need to ask. Just affirm your truth. Say to yourself, "I am loved and loving, I am happy, I am at peace," and God within confirms these truths by saying back to you, "Yes, you are!"

Shame hides. It lurks within your consciousness. When we shine the light of self-understanding on it, it scurries to a dark recess of the mind like a cockroach hiding from the light. But it's just a belief. It has no real power when we see it for what it is.

Chapter 9
Fantastic Furry Friends

1977: Late spring in West Central Illinois is almost as beautiful as all three of Charlie's angels combined. The residents of Macomb deserved a gorgeous spring. They'd earned it. The winter of 1976-1977 saw 54 inches of snow and was the third coldest winter on record. January was brutal, with an average temperature of ten degrees, and there were twelve days below zero that month. Deb was glad she'd installed that doggy door—there was no way she was going to venture out on those icy sidewalks to walk her buddy, no matter how adorable he was.

By mid-March, Uno felt like a convict walking out of prison after a lengthy stay. Sure, he had to venture out of the house twice daily to pee and poop, but by the time April finally dawned, he could finally get out and explore the neighborhood again. The month of May was perfect, with highs in the 70s and lows in the 40s.

Uno had to check on Jazzy, the black and brown terrier-beagle mix three doors down. Jazzy had a doggy door too, and Uno just needed to bark three or four times to get her out of the house. Sure enough, she was ready for an adventure. She came bounding through her door when Uno called her.

Like all the other dogs Uno had met, Jazzy's mind was free of thought but full of emotion. Uno still hoped to find another animal who could think and reason as he did but hadn't found one yet. Instinct and emotion ruled the minds of every dog, cat, raccoon, opossum, rabbit, and squirrel he'd met over the last year. Jazzy was easy to read. She was needy. But at the moment, Uno could tell she was grateful for the 70-degree afternoon temperatures too.

Uno felt sorry for Jazzy. She hadn't received much love from her first family, a businessman, and his wife. They ended up moving from Macomb to Chicago and decided not to take Jazzy. So, the Rudolph's, her forever family, gladly adopted her. Jazzy was trying to make up for all that lost love by seeking attention. Some dogs jump into a lap and quietly lie down. Not Jazzy. She demanded belly rubs and couldn't sit still on a lap—she wanted to be continuously stroked and caressed. Uno was her closest dog friend. He understood her desire for love.

Uno and Jazzy made their way down the alley between Carroll and Jackson streets. Their nostrils filled with canine scents. "Ah, I smell Brutus," thought Uno. Brutus, the chihuahua, had peed on this bush—and this shed—and this tree. "Brutus must drink plenty of water," thought Uno. A block later, they turned left and headed to the Bowen's house, where Brutus lived. It was a beautiful day, so Mrs. Bowen had tied up their manic friend in the back yard. The rope attached to his collar was secured to the clothesline so he could run back and forth across the yard in a straight line. As usual, he was wearing out the grass, running and barking to beat all hell. Brutus was a talker. He didn't listen well, but loved to bark—and bark, and bark, and bark.

Every little sound made Brutus jump and bark. Mrs. Bowen didn't need a doorbell. She had Brutus. Mr. Bowen repeatedly attempted to shush Brutus. He always failed. Their seven children gave Brutus lots of love and attention, but even that wasn't enough. It's as if Brutus was always shouting, "Hey! Look at me, listen to me!" After wrestling with Brutus for half an hour, Jazzy and Uno were off again.

They crossed brick laden Carroll Street to the Breeding family's two-story, Craftsman style home. Julie Breeding was a cute red-headed teenager who owned an all-black Maine Coon cat named Sherry Girl. Uno and Jazzy loved to harass that cat. Julie slept in a first-floor bedroom. Next to her bedroom window was a thickly padded window seat, Sherry Girl's favorite sleeping spot. "Aha, the window is open today," thought Uno. A flimsy screen was the only thing separating Sherry Girl from the two devious dogs.

Uno and Jazzy crept along the side of the house until they approached the large bush right outside the window. Sherry Girl was sound asleep. Uno led the charge, barking up a storm, and Jazzy chimed in. Sherry Girl shot straight up in the air and fell backward off the window seat. Jazzy and Uno looked at each other with big smiles on their faces. If they were human, they'd be high fiving each other and howling with laughter. Sherry Girl jumped back up on the window seat and peered down at the two morons. Her thick black fur stood high in the air as she let out a long, angry hiss and guttural growl. Bad doggies!

Sherry Girl curled up in a ball with her head next to the screen and gave a disapproving look at Jazzy and Uno. They backed up in the yard so they could see her better and barked up a storm. No reaction. If Sherry Girl could talk, Uno thought she would say, "Talk to the hand, dipsticks." She was fiercely independent. She didn't need any friends. The occasional head scratch was all she desired from Julie. Uno sensed that Sherry Girl lived in her head and was very happy there. She slept 14 hours a day and prowled through the Breeding's home at night. Uno and Jazzy grew tired of barking and being ignored, so they moved on.

They walked west on Carroll Street toward the Presbyterian church and crossed Dudley Street to Mr. Cunningham's house, a large, three-story Victorian house with a wrap-around porch. It harkened back to the turn of the century, probably the last time it had seen a coat of paint. Its large turret tower stood high and proud in the air, proclaiming its once youthful elegance. Ralphie, Mr. Cunningham's white Schnauzer, was sleeping on the screened-in back porch, his usual hang out. Poor Ralphie, he needed a friend.

Ralphie's previous owners abandoned him when he was a year old—they took him out to a country road and left him there. Grrrr—some people should never own a dog. Mr. Cunningham, a Biology teacher at Macomb High in his late twenties, found Ralphie while riding his 10-speed racing bike out on the back roads. But as much as he loved Ralphie, he was a busy guy. Mr. Cunningham was a good-looking bachelor and was usually out of the house—working, riding his bike, or out on a date. Ralphie was lonely and suffered from low self-worth.

Imagine being rejected, abandoned, and then ignored. Poor Ralphie.

Jazzy and Uno crept through the back porch's doggy door and found Ralphie asleep, lying on his thick pad next to the washing machine. His head jerked when he heard his friends, and he jumped up, so happy to see them. Jazzy and Uno greeted Ralphie by pouncing on him, and the three of them wrestled for several minutes. Uno could hear them laughing on the inside. The only thing dogs like more than human kisses and food is a good wrestling match. Ralphie led them into the kitchen, and the three of them feasted on the huge bowl of dry food that Mr. Cunningham always kept well stocked. Thank goodness for Ralphie that his owner never forgot to fill his large bowl every morning before leaving for work.

"Ugh! I'm so full," thought Uno. The three amigos decided it was mandatory nap time. They stumbled into the living room and jumped up on Mr. C's large, over-stuffed bean bag chair. "Ah, the life of a dog," thought Uno. Ralphie needed some love, so Uno flopped down next to him, laying his head across Ralphie's back. The three of them slept soundly, dreaming happy dog dreams— chasing squirrels and rabbits, enjoying belly rubs, and receiving unexpected gifts of bacon strips.

An hour later, there was a clicking sound at the front door. Mr. Cunningham was home! Uno and Jazzy leapt up and ran lickety-split toward the back porch. Uno stopped, turned, and gave Ralphie one last look and a big smile.

When Uno moseyed into the house later, Deb greeted him cheerfully.

"Hey, boy, where you been all day? Did you find a girlfriend?"

Uno chuckled to himself. "Nope, no girlfriends, but I do have some wonderful friends," he thought.

That night, as he lay in bed with Deb, Uno thought of his friends. He was grateful to have good buddies like Jazzy and Ralphie. Yes, Jazzy was a bit needy, and Ralphie was definitely lonely, but he loved them dearly, and they needed him. Uno thought of all the other dogs and cats in the neighborhood who weren't so lucky. Healthy friendships were not typical for some of them.

'Ol Brutus was just too self-involved, always talking and never listening. Sherry Girl was too independent, wanting nothing to do with others. Then there was Allie, a black lab who lived with the Vicks over on Calhoun Street. She was filled with fear because three other families had rejected her, so she was terrified of being left alone. Thumper, a pit bull who lived with Deb's friend Margaret, was too pushy and controlling. He never shared his ball and liked to keep Uno pinned to the ground when they wrestled.

Uno thought about human relationships and decided humans weren't that different from animals. Uno met many different kinds of people while exploring Macomb on his daily adventures. Some just didn't know what it took to have healthy relationships. "No," thought Uno. "It's not that they don't know, it's that many of them suffered through unhealthy, dysfunctional, and even cruel childhoods." Their early life experiences hadn't taught them how to create and maintain genuine and loving relationships.

Uno once sat with a man in the park who was very judgmental, always projecting his anger and judgment out onto the world. The man's thoughts gave Uno a glance at his childhood. He was raised by angry parents and hadn't received much love and encouragement. Kids need love to feel good about themselves.

One of Deb's friends, Sue, was a real know-it-all. She was intelligent, well read, and loved to pontificate about any subject. She sounded more like a teacher than a friend. She was full of opinions and beliefs and wasn't shy about pushing them on Deb. Not sharing them; but shoving them at her. Sue chose not to experience life in the present moment—her beliefs prevented her from seeing people and situations as they simply are. "Her beliefs are like a dirty window," Uno thought. "If only people knew how unnecessary most of their beliefs were, and how their beliefs mentally hold them back." Sue believed (and feared) that others thought of her as stupid or inept, so she overcompensated by trying to appear smart, opinionated, and full of conviction. Uno sensed that Sue's parents criticized her and made her feel *less than* when she was young.

Then there was June, another one of Deb's friends. Her parents didn't give her the essential love and kindness every parent should provide—they robbed her of a loving childhood. Uno could hear her thoughts clearly. She was in such pain. June's parents made her feel like she was too demanding and not worthy of their time. When June felt hurt and turned to one of her parents for understanding, they would usually take the side of the person who had hurt her. Receiving no validation from her parents made June believe that her feelings were insubstantial, and that she didn't matter. Because June felt so unacceptable to her parents, she had a hard time receiving love from others. On a conscious level, June felt like she should be lovable, but she would unconsciously dismiss others' expressions of love. June pushed people away and had few friends.

The common denominator for healthy relationships is love. People who have a hard time relating to others—they struggle with giving or receiving kindness, empathy, and compassion—are people who didn't receive enough love growing up.

Uno thought, "When we receive love and attention, we learn to love ourselves, and can then express that same love to others."

Uno was sure of the solution—self-love. He thought, "But it's challenging to generate self-love when you're under the hypnotic effects of your own false beliefs. Great accomplishments are rarely accomplished alone." Uno thought about something he had heard Deb mention to a client concerning a compassionate, loving, and service-oriented organization, Alcoholics Anonymous.

"This organization was God-originated," thought Uno. Its emphasis is simple: People helping people, based on a foundation of spiritual principles. "Just like A.A.," thought Uno, "We could all benefit by helping each other take inventory of and clearing out our non-loving thoughts, false beliefs, and hurtful memories—to clean off that dirty window."

"Most importantly," thought Uno, "We can learn about and get closer to that inner God presence. Too many people are unaware of their divine self—that presence within that loves us deeply, that comforts us, guides us, and helps us forgive others and ourselves."

So, Uno decided to do his part, right then and there. As he drifted off to sleep, he planted new seeds into the Universe.

"I know for all my dog and cat friends, for all the people I've met, for anyone struggling with unhealthy and dysfunctional relationships, and for all people everywhere, that we are loved beyond our imagination. A Perfect Universal Power that is within us and all around us exudes Life to us. This Life is Love. Life is Love and Love is Life. The energy that animates a flower, elephant, or child is the same energy that unites people in loving and friendly relationships. I know for all people that we love ourselves deeply. We are willing and able to release from our consciousness all thoughts and beliefs that seemingly oppose love: fear, anger, judgment, disappointment, shame, guilt, rejection, abandonment, inattentiveness, cruelty, negation, a false sense of separation, low self-image, competition, the desire to be right; all thoughts that seemingly separate us from our inner True Self and each other. As everyone sees these misperceptions for what they are, our self-love grows and blossoms. We treat ourselves with loving kindness, we are gentle with ourselves, and we see the world as open to all possibilities. As this love grows in our collective consciousness, we express it to everyone in our lives. We are open to new ideas. We think about and take action on behalf of the needs and wants of others. We are kind, light-hearted, positive, respectful, optimistic, and accepting of all. We are a fountain of love, bursting forth with positive energy, and people are attracted to this energy. We create a cornucopia of friendships and healthy relationships. I give thanks for this truth about humankind that flows through me at this moment, and I release and firmly secure these words into the Law of Cause and Effect, knowing that they manifest and multiply exponentially. And, so it is."

Here are a few **truth affirmations** and random thoughts related to *creating and maintaining loving relationships and loving ourselves in the process*. They are written in the first-person voice just for you and are "Uno-approved."

- I care about my friends. I ask them how they're doing, and how they feel. I'm sincerely interested.
- I am open, honest, and transparent when communicating with my friends.
- The trust that I've earned in my friendships is sacred. I am honest with my friends.
- I'm a good listener.
- I respect my friends' boundaries. I'm not needy or clingy.
- I like myself. I'm happy when I'm alone.
- I call and text my friends just to ask them how they're doing.
- I don't judge my friends. I accept them as they are.
- I support my friends. I'm their biggest cheerleader.
- I forgive easily and avoid putting expectations on my friends.
- I love myself, so I don't let others take advantage of me.
- I acknowledge my mistakes and apologize if I've hurt someone.
- I allow my friends to vent without trying to fix them.
- I never talk behind a friend's back. I am a loyal friend.
- I give my friends my complete attention.
- I don't try to change my friends. I don't "should" on them.
- I allow my friends to express their feelings without judgment. I am compassionate.
- I empathize with my friends. I share their pain, and I don't look down on them.
- I respect differences in my relationships.
- I add goodness and kindness to the lives of my friends.
- I avoid competing with my friends. I let them be right and don't try to control.
- I compliment my friends easily and often.
- I give my friends my time, and I'm always there for them when they need me.

- My friendships are fun-ships. Laughter is mandatory.
- I refuse to hold grudges. I forgive easily without being a doormat.
- I like expressing care and concern more than proving a point.
- I don't give advice unless I'm asked.
- I am available to my friends during their tough times.
- When a friend and I disagree, I don't take it personally.
- I encourage my friends to grow.
- I let go of all desire for power or status in my friendships. I am gentle with my words and behavior.
- I make my friends feel good about themselves. I honor their interests and achievements with recognition and praise.
- I "suit up and show up" when my friends need me.
- I am consistent in communicating with my friends, whether it be in person, on the phone, via text message, or on social media—I don't wait for them to make contact, I reach out.
- I am always thinking of new things to do with my friends, so the relationship doesn't get stale or too routine.
- I express to my friends how much I value and admire specific character traits. I look for ways to do this in front of others, in an authentic way.
- I am vocal about my needs. I know my friends can't read my mind.
- I like to make small gestures of kindness to my friends. I love surprising them with acts of love.

Rhyming Affirmations

I am open and honest in all my communication,
It elevates my friendships to a higher vibration.

I don't judge my friends. I accept them as they are,
I treat them like they're a Hollywood movie star.

I champion my friends, and I'm their biggest backer,
I do this with gusto 'cause I'm no slacker.

When I mess up, I apologize and make amends,
This authentic practice pays big dividends.

I never gossip, I am true and loyal,
I treat my friends as if they're a British royal.

I listen to my friends and give them my respect,
Our minds become aligned, we blend, we connect.

I empathize with my friends, and I feel their pain,
Empathy is essential when they're on rocky terrain.

If my friends and I were identical, that would be boring,
Differences are good, they keep me from snoring.

When my friends need help, I'm right there for 'em,
I do this because I care. Oh hell, I adore 'em.

I am generous with my compliments and expressions of care,
I'm creative with compliments. I love others with flair.

Uno's Random Thoughts

Being a good friend to others starts with feeling good about yourself. The same is true regarding intimate relationships. A solid relationship begins with other-centeredness, integrity, loyalty, commitment, and kindness. These qualities are scarce in someone who's self-centered, fearful, judgmental, or lacking in self-worth. Self-love is the foundation of good relationships.

Giving to others without a hint of expectation or condition is godlike. Think about it. That's what Spirit does, consistently and continuously—gives, gives, gives.

Empathy is an admirable quality in a true friend. Allowing a friend to pour out their feelings, to bitch and moan, to tell their story and share their pain—without interruption, without advice, and without a solution—this is genuine empathy. Sometimes we just need someone to be there with us.

Be willing to work through conflict with your friends. Forgiving is an act of love, to your friends and yourself. I'm not talking about forgiving someone for killing one of your parents, that's major league forgiveness. I'm talking about forgiving them for making a judgmental remark, disagreeing with one of your precious beliefs, standing you up, or for not supporting you when you need them. Let it go. Don't take it personally. A *self-centered* person takes every slight personally, an *other-centered* person understands that people make mistakes and are doing the best they can. Forgiveness is the cornerstone of a solid relationship.

Chapter 10
Lack is Wack

It was early August in Macomb and temperatures were climbing. The TV weatherman on WGEM—the old guy with a huge head and darting eyes—said that highs would be in the low 100s. Worse than that, the humidity was so thick that there was a run on deodorant at Eagle's Supermarket. On days like this, Uno liked to either stay indoors and enjoy the air conditioning or sit in the blow-up kiddie pool under the large elm tree in the back yard. Deb loved lounging in that pool with her transistor radio and two or three cans of cold Busch beer.

That evening, all hell broke loose. A violent thunderstorm descended on West Central Illinois, and the house was shaking from the wind. Deb sat in front of the TV, listening for tornado warnings, and Uno was curled up next to her. Unlike most dogs, the rumbling and crackling thunder didn't scare Uno. Jazzy and Ralphie were probably shaking like leaves, hiding under a bed, but Uno knew it was just a storm. He stayed close to Deb to calm *her* fear.

Boom! A large flash of lightning lit up the darkened house! Crack! Thud! Something hammered down on the roof above the adjacent dining room, shattering the window next to the dining room table. Glass flew across the table and floor, the wind howled loudly through the house, and rain sprayed into the dining room. Deb's entire body jerked, and she peed her pants a little. She sprang off the couch with a jolt, lost her footing, and fell on the living room floor. Uno jumped off the couch and ran to her side.

"Are you okay, Deb?!" he thought. "Are you hurt?"

Deb leapt to her feet and ran toward the dining room. Uno saw that she was barefoot. "The glass!" thought Uno, as he barked loudly several times. Deb turned and looked at him as he grabbed one of her sandals in his mouth and ran toward her.

"My God, that dog is smart," thought Deb. She took the sandal from Uno's mouth, slipped it on, and ran to pick up the other sandal.

"Thanks, boy. You saved me a trip to the emergency room."

Deb ran into the dining room, glass crunching beneath her sandals. The rain pelted the table and rug. There was nothing she could do to stop it. The wind was overpowering, howling through the window. Deb turned and ran upstairs, Uno followed at a fast clip. She flew into the guest room, stripped the double bed quickly, and grunted as she heaved the mattress off the frame, dragging it out the door and down the hallway. She tripped while running down the stairs and fell on top of the mattress as it sailed down to the landing. Uno thought it was funny that during all this chaos, Deb screamed, "Wheeeee!" as she rode the mattress down the stairs.

Deb grabbed the side handles of the mattress again and dragged it quickly to the window. She leaned it against the hole in her house and fell against it. The rain stopped spraying into the room.

"Wow! That was intense! Whaddaya think, Uno?!"

Uno crouched in the living room, agitated and out of breath. He barked repeatedly and jumped up and down. Uno wanted so badly to lean against that mattress with Deb but was cautious of the glass on the floor.

Deb stood and leaned into the mattress for what seemed like an eternity but was probably about an hour. Finally, the wind died down, but it was still raining. Deb had dozed off, still leaning against the mattress. She looked like she was asleep on a vertical bed. Uno barked.

Deb jolted awake. She looked around the room. "Did we survive, boy?"

The next morning, Deb was on the phone to Gregg, a friend and local contractor. She had dropped her homeowner's insurance several months ago when they raised the premiums but had neglected to buy a new policy. She was regretting that bonehead decision now. Gregg paid a visit that afternoon to assess the damage. From what Uno could gather, a tree fell on the roof, and Deb was looking at a $4,000 expense, even with the friend discount Gregg was offering.

"Shit, shit, shit, shit, SHIT!" Deb was upset. Gregg tried to console her by reminding her how grateful she should be for escaping injury and incurring a mountain of medical expenses. It didn't work. She spent the rest of the day in an irritated mood, seeking advice from friends on the phone.

"I can't cash in my bank CDs," Deb whined to her friend Karen. "They're finally earning some good interest, and I'd take a nasty hit in penalties for early withdrawal. I'm going to need that money when I'm on a fixed income fifteen years from now. I don't want to subsist on peanut butter and jelly when I'm seventy-five. I guess I'll have to take out a home improvement loan at the bank to pay Gregg, so there's another monthly bill. I just don't know what I'm going to do," she said to Karen.

"How about a part-time job to earn some cash?" offered Karen.

"Haha, good one, Karen. I work about 50 hours a week at the clinic as it is. Besides, I'm too old to be delivering pizza or flippin' burgers."

Deb let loose a long sigh. Uno could tell she was close to tears. He jumped up on the couch with her and nuzzled into her chest. Deb hugged Uno tightly as she said goodbye to Karen and hung up the phone.

"Oh, Uno, what are we gonna do? I might have to start buying the cheap dog food for you. I just hope I don't have to eat it too."

Uno had never heard Deb talk like this. She was full of fear. Over what? Money? Uno thought about Deb's fear, and he realized it was grounded in a deep-seated belief she'd held all her life—a belief in the ideas of lack and limitation. Deb made several more phone calls that day. Uno wished she would stop. She was only strengthening her beliefs.

Deb called her friend Betty Jo to tell her the thunderstorm story. Betty Jo countered with an account of her own about her dental bills. She needed a root canal, a bridge, and three cavities filled. Betty Jo was looking at a $700 dental bill, money she just didn't have in her savings. "I'm thinking about having two of my teeth pulled," said Betty Jo. "That would cost $300 less, for God's sake!" By the time Deb finished that call, she was even more depressed.

Then Deb called her friend Joan, who told Deb about her '68 Ford Falcon needing some major engine work. Joan said she didn't have the money for a new car, or even a used one, but couldn't afford the $800 estimate she'd received from "Red" down at the garage. She was considering walking for a few months until she could save the money. That call cheered Deb right up.

The entire afternoon was a feeding frenzy. Deb and her friends were gobbling up each other's fear like a group of buzzards devouring a fresh buffalo carcass. This madness HAD to stop! Uno began thinking of ways to divert Deb's attention and energy away from all these limiting thoughts. Her friends were not helping, so Uno knew he must.

Uno spent the rest of the afternoon lying in the back yard, thinking. He thought about the spiritual principles and ideas underlying this idea of universal abundance, about the many forms of prosperity, about the quality of diversity within the Oneness, and about a concept he had taught other souls about on multiple occasions in the afterlife—Infinite Potential.

That last idea, Infinite Potential, was intriguing. For Uno, human words were very limiting, so he thought hard and came up with this:

There is a substance or energy field that permeates and surrounds the material world and all life forms, existing at all points of space throughout the universe. It is entirely neutral, receptive, malleable, and creative. Contemporary physicists are getting closer in their understanding of it—they call it a unified field, part of scientists' exploration into quantum field theory. They are referring to it as the reality of the non-material. Uno thought of this energy field as spiritual soil. The energy field receives a seed—a thought—and the soil acts on the seed to grow something. Uno knew that the key to understanding this creative medium was dependent on the unification of the studies of science, spirituality, philosophy, and psychology. Each of these bodies of knowledge is a piece of the puzzle. Seeing the complete picture of the puzzle requires the joining of humankind's knowledge.

On a human level, the seeds planted into this universal energy field are thoughts. We create our reality from the inside out with our thoughts. Every human-made object we see in our world once started as a single thought. Inherent in this energy field is Infinite Potential, the idea that creating anything is possible. Uno thought of the ultimate example: An advanced soul named Jesus created loaves of bread and fish out of thin air. The loaves and fish were instantly created from this energy field by a powerful thought seed planted by Jesus. To a spiritually advanced soul like Jesus or the Buddha, the notion that Jesus' actions were some type of magic or miracle is amusing; Jesus knew it was simple spiritual science. He called it "great faith."

Uno thought about how these spiritual principles applied to Deb and her perceived lack of abundance. Deb was creating without even knowing it, and she was creating what she *didn't* want—lack and limitation. Uno knew that what we put our attention on, and give energy to, is what we create, whether we realize it or not, or want it or not. Deb's thoughts about not having enough money, of not being able to pay bills, and having to do without are potent thoughts, and push abundance and prosperity away from her. These types of limiting thoughts are not just obstacles. They are like a shield that prevents the universe from giving Deb what she actually wanted: money.

So, Uno knew what his role was in this little Deb drama. He needed to know universal truth for her. This thought gave Uno peace and closure, so he drifted off to a deep sleep as he lay in the back yard. Two hours later, Big Tom strolled by and saw Uno lying there. Big Tom was the nickname Uno had given an unneutered blonde tomcat who prowled the neighborhood. He was all muscle, weighing nearly 20 pounds, and had sired half the kittens in a ten-block radius.

Big Tom wasn't afraid of anything. He approached Uno, gave him a sniff, and then lifted his leg and peed on Uno's hindquarters. Uno awoke instantly, thinking it was raining. He smelled cat urine. He jumped to his feet and saw Tom standing four feet away. The tomcat had a menacing look on his face, daring Uno to fight. Uno took a step forward, and Big Tom raised his back and let out a long, low growl. Uno stepped back. The last thing he wanted was a body full of cuts and gouges from this small cougar.

Uno retreated a few more steps and then turned and ran. Big Tom gave chase, howling up a storm as he ran. Uno was terrified now. Big Tom was catching up to Uno, ready to pounce.

Ka-splash! Uno belly flopped into the kiddie pool, which was full, from last night's rain. Big Tom stopped so fast he almost toppled over. Uno quickly turned around and used his hind legs to splash Big Tom with dirty rainwater. The irritated bully turned and ran. Big Tom wasn't afraid. He just detested getting wet.

Dirty rainwater was better than cat pee. Yuck! Uno leaned against the side of the plastic pool and rubbed his butt and back vigorously. "Whoa, that water is cold!" thought Uno. He quickly jumped out of the pool, shook himself off, and ran into the house. Deb was busy in the kitchen.

"What are you DOING, Uno? You're soaking wet!"

Uno gave Deb a sad look and hung his head.

"Awww, come 'ere boy." Deb grabbed a towel from the laundry basket on the kitchen table and knelt, rubbing Uno from top to bottom."

"Rub my butt some more," thought Uno. "Get that nasty smell off me!"

"Jesus Christ on a pogo stick! What did you roll in? You smell like a turd with bad breath!"

Before Uno knew what was happening, Deb scooped him up and carried him to the large kitchen sink. She made sure the water was nice and warm and then squirted him thoroughly with Lemon Joy. Uno loved a good bath. Deb was so kind and gentle with him, massaging those soapsuds deep into his fur. She always made sure she didn't get any in his eyes or mouth.

"That warm water from the faucet sprayer feels so good. I love you so much, Deb," thought Uno.

Deb treated herself to some comfort food for supper—grilled hamburgers, medium rare, and homemade fries. Uno loved Deb's burgers. She always cooked two for her best bud.

It was a lazy TV night. Deb and Uno snuggled up on the sofa and watched their favorite Sunday night shows. *The Wonderful World of Disney*, *The Six Million Dollar Man*, and then *All in the Family* and *Alice*, followed by Uno's absolute fave, *The Carol Burnett Show*. By the time Carol sang, "I'm so glad we had this time together..." Deb was snoring.

"Come on, Deb, time for bed!" Uno licked Deb's face three or four times, laughing to himself. She gently shoved his face from hers.

"All right, all right, I'm awake." Deb stood up unsteadily and several kernels of popcorn fell off her shirt. She knew it was time for bed when the local news came on. As she said to herself a thousand times, "Nope, not watching THAT crap."

Uno spooned with Deb in bed that night, but she lay awake for the longest time. Uno could hear her thoughts. Bills, bank loan, interest rate too high, things she wasn't buying, no vacation this year. Fear, lack, fear, lack, fear, lack. She finally drifted off to sleep—a herky-jerky, frustrated sleep.

Uno slowly rose and repositioned himself, laying his snout directly across the back of Deb's head. He meditated for 30 minutes, at first focusing on his breath, and then centering himself firmly in the Oneness of All. Uno knew his thought-seeds needed to be powerful, and buried deep into the One Mind, that Deb shared. He knew he needed extra emotion in this healing prayer. His intense feeling was like a fire from within.

"I am centered in the One Mind, completely immersed and saturated in this loving and creative Universal Power. It is who I am. I live within it and I am made of it. I am here, within this Infinite Universal Intelligence, and it within me. We are One. In this oneness, I speak my word for Deb. I know for her that she is whole, perfect, and complete, exactly as she is. She lacks nothing to be the perfect soul that she is—pure, innocent, and open to universal truth. I know for Deb that she lovingly releases from her mind thoughts or beliefs based in fear, lack, limitation, frustration, chaos, uncertainty, or doubt. She knows in her heart that these misperceptions are lies disguised as reality. I know for Deb that she stops miscreating her reality with these lower thoughts. They are gone, now! If they return, she acknowledges their deceit and washes them away from her mind. I know for Deb that she is one hundred percent certain of her divine nature. She knows she is a powerfully creative child of a universal Power and Presence. Like God, she is god-like, and she uses her birthright power to create the life she wants. I know for Deb that she knows, beyond all doubt, that Universal Abundance is not something to get, but is who she is. She is abundance in expression. Prosperity flows to and from her with ease and grace, in the form of money, time, gifts, people, wisdom, love, peace, and a multitude of wonderful and fulfilling opportunities. Deb is on the same vibrational level of that which she desires. What she wants, she already is, and she knows this with strong certainty. With a grateful, loving heart, I give thanks to All-That-Is for this truth about Deb. It is certain, it is done, I know it. Thank you, Mother, Father, God. And, so it is."

Uno was confident that his word had power, but as yet had not seen many manifestations of it. Tim, Deb's brother, was the exception. His entire attitude and outlook on life had changed. He was much more upbeat and optimistic these days. Uno knew Mr. Welker was still alive and that Crystal was happier, but he hadn't seen Chilly around town or the others he'd met and prayed for over the last year.

Deb was Uno's roommate, so Uno was privy to every aspect of her thought life. Uno was not shocked, but surprisingly pleased, when Deb's life changed dramatically in late 1977.

Deb was doing her annual fall cleaning when she found her dad's files in the attic. When her father passed in 1960, she had collected his private papers to review, but they had been collecting dust in her attic ever since. Deep inside a side pocket of her dad's leather briefcase, she found a wad of cloth. It was a handkerchief wrapped around several layers of tinfoil. She unwrapped the package carefully, and within the foil was a single baseball card. It was a 1952 Topps brand baseball card featuring the one and only Mickey Mantle. Deb didn't know anything about baseball cards, but she thought it might be valuable since her father had painstakingly protected it.

Her abundance journey began with Rory Bienenstock, an antique and junk dealer in Macomb. Rory put Deb in contact with Mr. Guy Franklyn, who owned a sports memorabilia shop in Chicago. A month later, Deb sat through a six-hour-long auction in New York City. Finally, her card went up for bid. Eighteen bids later, the card sold for $38,000. After fees and taxes, she took home $26,000. Half went to Tim. Deb needed $4,500 for her storm-damaged home repairs and ended up with $13,000. Coincidence? Uno knew better.

Here are a few **truth affirmations** and random thoughts related to *growing an Abundance Consciousness*. They are written in the first-person voice just for you and are "Uno-approved."

- My life is filled with abundance.
- God is abundant. I am made of God stuff, therefore I am abundant.
- Prosperity flows to me easily and effortlessly in the form of money, gifts, time, health, and wonderful opportunities.
- I am a prosperity magnet.
- I let go of the idea that other people's prosperity and success hinders mine.
- Like grains of sand on a beach, the universe is limitless. I let go of all thoughts and beliefs related to lack and limitation.
- I am more than just ready and open to attracting abundance. I attract abundance. Period.
- I am vibrating at the same frequency as the prosperity I attract.
- I am joyfully floating in a sea of abundance.
- I deserve all the goodness that the universe has to offer.
- Abundance is my birthright based on my true identity—a creative spiritual being.
- My eyes are open to the abundance that surrounds me. It is mine, I am it.
- Thank you for the prosperity that shows up in my life in many different forms.
- Prosperity is drawn to me like metal shavings to a magnet.
- I expect to receive more abundance in my life. It is a given.
- I see that the idea of lack is a lie. I banish this false thought from my mind and know that my potential is unlimited.
- I celebrate the abundance of others and say, "Yes, that's for me!"
- I let go of any thoughts or beliefs related to critical judgment or jealousy of other people's prosperity,

knowing that there's more than enough of everything for everyone.

- I know that loving money and leading a life of integrity and value are not in opposition. That which I love, desire, place my continued attention on, and work hard for will show up in my life, in accordance with the Divine Law of Cause and Effect.
- Every time I think of unlimited abundance, I am making myself more receptive to it.
- I am one with an unlimited supply of abundance, potential, and possibility. I align my mind with this invisible universal substance, this divine energy that fills every cell and atom.
- My potential knows no boundaries or limits. Everything is possible in this generous universe governed by divine law.
- Prosperity thinks of me as enticing and alluring because I praise and celebrate that which I love and enjoy.
- I am open to new and positive changes in my life. I AM positive change.
- I love, relish, adore, cherish, and savor everyone in my life and all that I give and receive. My love and gratitude, like my potential, is unlimited.
- I am happy for the success and prosperity of others because they show me the generosity of the universe.
- I know that I am more than enough, exactly as I am, and give thanks for the continued blessings that rush to embrace me.
- I know that as I radiate with gratitude, abundance says, "There you are!"
- Health and wealth flow through my life like a raging river.
- I give and I receive. I am an active and grateful hub of the Law of Circulation.
- Something wonderful is happening through me right now, right here.
- Everywhere I look, I see abundance.
- I know there is a spiritual energy that is everywhere present in the universe. This divine substance responds to my thoughts and creates that which I put my energy,

emotion, and focus on. I use it to create that which I desire.

- What I want, wants me. What I love, loves me. What I focus on, focuses on me.
- I know that abundance and prosperity begin in my mind and are activated by emotion and desire.
- I am in line. I am not waiting. I am in line with prosperity.
- Unexpected income is searching for me. "Here I am, good-looking!"
- The universe conspires to provide me with what I need and want.

Rhyming Affirmations

I am abundance, I am wealth, I am prosperity,
I know this now with the utmost clarity.

Abundance and I are on the same vibration,
My thought-seeds are the source of this awesome creation.

Abundance is an ocean, and I'm riding its wave,
I surf on down to all that I crave.

Lack and limitation, man, what a lie,
The universe is generous with its endless supply.

I'm never jealous of other people's prosperity,
I say, "Yes, that's for me" with persistent regularity.

Life is unlimited, it has no ceiling,
This universal truth gives me a warm fuzzy feeling.

Abundance sees me as enticing and alluring,
Its love for me is comforting and reassuring.

I am a perfect creation of a Perfect Creator,
Lack and limitation? Ha! See ya later, alligator.

Abundance is my birthright, not just something to obtain,
When I'm sure of this fact, I have everything to gain.

Everywhere I look, I see a multitude of plenty,
Look, under my foot. Yep, that's a twenty.

Uno's Random Thoughts

Many young people today refer to themselves as spiritual but not religious. Unknown to many of them, and the majority of the earth's population, are a group of new religious faiths referred to as New Thought. At the dawn of the 20th century, these new, rebellious philosophies were referred to as Mental Science or Practical Christianity. Their ideas have their roots in the most profound ancient thinkers—Socrates, Plato, Aristotle, Heraclitus, Lao Tzu, Marcus Aurelius, the Buddha, Jesus, Rumi, Hafiz. Contemporary mystics espouse the same ideas as these ancient thinkers in new ways. They talk about our innate ability to change effects, conditions, and life circumstances using the power of the mind. Most people would agree with this statement: "If you think you're going to fail, you probably will." On the other hand, many people would snicker at this statement: "If you know beyond a doubt that you are abundance in expression, you will attract more abundance." But they are essentially the same idea.

Spirituality and philosophy are now intersecting with psychology and physical science. We are living in a new and exciting era. Positive thinking and mental visualizations, which sports psychologists have been touting for years to improve athlete's performance, are used for a variety of purposes—healing diseases, manifesting material objects, enhancing confidence and self-esteem, increasing peace of mind, or attracting prosperity. We have learned to hone and focus our minds not just to feel good, or to hit a home run, but to attract and create specific objects, circumstances, and conditions. Weird? Not really. Jesus taught and mastered this divine Law of Cause and Effect and then said everyone else could too, but that particular Bible passage is often overlooked. If you're interested in the Bible, look it up: John 14:12.

The Law of Cause and Effect is exacting and doesn't play favorites. Like the Law of Gravity, it doesn't care if you're Catholic, Jewish, Presbyterian, or atheist. It simply responds to mental energy. That's why someone who is seemingly evil, like Hitler, could have such a profound effect on the world. Hitler had great mental strength and passion. What he desired, he put his attention and focus on, coupled with intense feeling. He changed minds, he changed circumstances, and he manifested evil. Jesus, Mother Teresa, and Gandhi used the same law to produce very different effects. The Law of Cause and Effect responded to them all equally. This is the same law we use to attract more abundance, in a variety of forms, into our lives.

Dr. Wayne Dyer turned the phrase, "I will believe it when I see it" upside down. He wrote, "I will see it when I believe it." A phrase like this makes us exclaim, "Ahhh, what an interesting notion!" Each of us has an intuitive radar for universal truth. Some truth detectors are more in tune or experienced, which is another way of saying we are all at varying levels or stages of spiritual development. One level is not any better than another, just as the sixth grade is not better than the first grade. It took humankind thousands of years to discover the Law of Attraction, and yet this idea is timeless. Within the last 50 years, hundreds of books have been written about this new spiritual law. Now it's referred to as *The Secret*. The ancient Law of Attraction has much to teach us about attracting prosperity into our lives.

The 1950s were the heyday of door-to-door sales. There's an old story about two mobile salesmen that goes something like this: The first salesman thought he could sell fifty units per month. He knew he could sell anything; he believed it firmly. You could say he had faith in himself. This salesman routinely sold fifty units per month. In contemporary language, we would say he has an abundance consciousness. The second salesman had less confidence and lower self-esteem. He expected to sell twenty units per month. He routinely sold twenty units per month. We get what we expect. As Jesus said, "It is done unto you as you believe." Psychologists have performed scores of social experiments confirming this idea. We think of this phenomenon as purely mental. What most of us don't understand is that mental equals spiritual, and that there are invisible spiritual laws that govern our reality similar to the invisible physical laws we accept as fact. But we're gaining in our understanding. We are evolving.

Deb's kindness knew no bounds. She didn't hesitate to say, "Yes!" when Jeff Radcliff, the county director of child and family services, phoned and asked her to foster a teenage boy. Jeff and Deb had been classmates at Western Illinois University a quarter of a century ago, and they were both happy when their jobs and lives occasionally intersected.

The young man's story was tragic. Jacob was 16 years old and disabled. When he was 12, he lost the lower half of his right leg in a car accident. Three days ago, he lost both his parents in another car accident, a head-on collision that occurred on one of those, "damn two-lane highways in Western Illinois," as Deb called them. Jacob had been in the back seat of the car and escaped serious injury. To complicate matters, Jacob's parents, both in their early fifties, had no siblings or living parents. Jacob was the final branch on his family tree.

Jeff chose Deb for this delicate task because of her counseling skills and experience, as well as her big heart. Young Jacob would need all the loving he could get. When Uno heard Deb talking on the phone about their new roommate, he couldn't contain his excitement. The following day, Jacob arrived at Deb's house.

Jacob was tall for a 16-year-old, standing six feet, two inches. A mop of long, ash-blonde curly hair fell over his bright green eyes and surrounded his head like a helmet. Deb would later remark that he had the most engaging smile and brightest teeth. When Jacob smiled, everyone smiled, she would say. He had a swimmer's build, thin and a broad, muscled chest. Jacob was on the MHS swim team despite only possessing one and a half legs. He had a prosthetic leg and foot, the latter covered with an Adidas sneaker. He had mastered his artificial limb years ago and walked with just a slight limp.

"Jacob, I'd like you to meet my best friend in the world, Uno."

Jacob knelt to greet Uno and Uno pounced on Jacob, sending him reeling backward on the carpet. Uno gave Jacob's face an enthusiastic face bath as Jacob laughed loudly, hugging his new friend.

"I've always wanted a hairy friend," laughed Jacob. "My parents would never let me have a dog." Jacob's face turned downward for an instant.

"Well, you've got one now," exclaimed Deb. "Come on, let me show you to your room."

Over the next few weeks, Jacob had an uneasy adjustment. At times, it seemed he was feeling happy and upbeat, but the next day he would be silent again. Imagine losing both your mom and dad the same day, instantly, and never being able to see their faces again. The transition was stressful one day and grueling the next. Deb encouraged Jacob to talk about his folks and his feelings. He told Deb he believed in an afterlife, although he doubted it was in the clouds with wings and harps. So she urged Jacob to talk to his parents since their souls were "out there somewhere." Talking to them was difficult at first, but as time went by, this daily ritual helped Jacob immensely.

Deb's favorite phrase to Jacob was, "Don't believe that crap about men not crying. You lost your mom and dad, it's normal to cry your eyes out." She also encouraged daily hugs and as much social interaction as Jacob was up for, and she made sure he never missed a swim team practice. Keeping him on a routine was important. Uno helped as well. He slept with Jacob every night, and affirmatively prayed for peace, happiness, love, and gratitude for Jacob.

The most potent healing medicine for Jacob was the help he gave others. As they say in A.A., "get out of your head and help others." Part of Deb's job was assisting the county's social workers. Twice weekly, she would accompany them on their home visits. Many of the county's clients needed counseling in addition to the services provided by the social workers. Deb received permission from the administrator to include Jacob on her visits to people with disabilities or physical challenges. Deb called them "kindness ride-alongs," and Jacob loved them. Uno did too. Deb didn't ask permission to bring Uno—she just brought him.

One of their first visits was to Roger, a 27-year-old construction worker who lost the use of his legs due to massive spinal damage after falling from a three-story scaffolding. Like grief and death, people move through psychological stages before accepting their disability—denial, anger, bargaining, depression, and acceptance. Roger was somewhere between bargaining and depression, actually vacillating between the two. He would say, "I would give anything to have my legs back" (bargaining) and then realize that wasn't possible and fall into a depression.

Jacob told Roger about his own experiences. He was a natural, not preachy or formal in any way, just telling his story and then summarizing what he'd learned about himself. He told Roger about his realization that he was not his body and talked about feeling so much more human now than before he lost his leg. Jacob talked about focusing on what he could do with his new body and not what he couldn't do. Roger's eyes lit up momentarily when Jacob said, "The hell with limitations, I'm going to do what I want to do, not what anyone else, or even a voice in my head, tells me I can or can't do."

Uno was a natural healer too. He was always paying attention to discussions and offering love when there was a call for it—his head in a lap, a tongue bath, a whimper, or merely leaning against someone's leg. Uno instinctively knew the kind of comfort and compassion people needed.

Judy worked at the Princess Shoppe. She was a 58-year-old hairstylist, one of the best in Macomb. She recently lost most of her eyesight over a three-month period because of a rare retinal disease. She could no longer work and was utterly dependent on her daughter, Dianne. Judy was stuck in stage two, anger. She was bitchy and irritable most of the day, and Dianne was beginning to tire of her attitude, which made matters worse. Frustration, anger, outburst, guilt, apologies, silence—it was a daily cycle driving them both nuts.

Jacob knew about anger. He remembered how pissed off he'd been when he lost his leg. He met Judy's anger head-on with his own.

"I can't even see my hair in the mirror. This sucks!"

"Yeah, I remember how I felt when I realized I couldn't play basketball or football for the rest of my friggin' life! That sucked, big time!"

"I hate my life!" screamed Judy.

"Yeah, screw this shit, goddammit! Let's beat somebody up, Judy! Come on! I'll hold their arms behind their back, and you punch 'em! I'll help you make sight adjustments if you miss!"

Uno jumped up and down, barking.

Judy cocked her head, shocked and confused. Jacob chuckled, and the two of them burst into laughter. Then Judy burst into tears. She was moving closer to acceptance a little more each day. Listening to Jacob and talking to Deb helped to speed up the process. Judy later said the two of them were like a mirror held to her face—she could see herself more clearly.

Over the next two months, Jacob helped several other people. Eighty-three-year-old Bill had Parkinson's disease. He could no longer drive and had a hard time accepting this perceived limitation. Nine-year-old Yasmina was in the beginning stages of muscular dystrophy. Fifty-three-year-old Betty had her foot amputated due to circulatory issues related to diabetes. Sixty-two-year-old Susie was recovering from a stroke. Jacob intuitively knew what to say to each of them and when to say it. Deb was amazed. Uno could see what a difference helping to heal others made on Jacob's self-confidence and outlook as he moved through his grief.

By the time Christmas 1977 rolled around, Jacob was needed at home. Deb had tripped on an area rug in the dining room and fell headfirst against a serving table. She earned a large lump on her forehead but wasn't seriously hurt. When she fell, though, the table toppled over and landed on Uno's paw, breaking a bone. Jacob came hobbling down the stairs at Daytona speed when he heard Uno cry out in pain. The sound of a dog yelping and crying makes people move with lightning-fast urgency. Poor Uno. Now *he* was disabled.

Christmas morning was not as much fun unless you could roll around in a pile of torn and discarded wrapping paper and chew on ribbons and bows. Well, that's what Uno thought anyway. Tim, Deb, and Jacob seemed to be enjoying themselves. The three of them savored a breakfast of cinnamon French toast, eggs, and bacon, and were now sipping their coffee, ready to dig into the mountain of gifts under the tree. The fire was crackling, and the sound of Andy Williams Christmas music was crooning from the Hi-Fi stereo set. Uno was treated to several pieces of crunchy bacon as he lay on his new, temporary throne, a thick, soft pile of blankets on the floor next to the sofa.

"What a wonderful, love-filled, precious moment this Christmas morning is," thought Uno. "I'm taking a mental snapshot of it, so I'll always have it with me."

Uno was growing accustomed to being served, but he didn't like being immobile, especially when he had to pee. Thank God Deb understood his tinkle signal, a gentle whine. She would carry Uno out the back door and hold him upright to keep the weight off his broken paw while he took a leak. What a pain. Uno detested being dependent on others and making them work so hard for him. Deb or Jacob carried him to pee and poop and lugged him upstairs to sleep. They loved loving Uno, but he didn't care one bit for being a burden.

"Perhaps this guilt I feel is my emotional reaction to my disability," thought Uno. "I don't think I went through a denial stage. My leg is broken, so I can't deny that. I'm not really angry. What's the point? I don't think I've been bargaining, although I'd trade some dog kisses for more of that bacon. Depression isn't really in my nature. I'm too grateful to be depressed. So, I guess I've accepted my disability. Of course, knowing that it's temporary makes it much easier to accept."

Uno thought about all the people with disabilities he'd met over the last few months, about his own vulnerability with this thick bandage wrapped around his paw, and about his new pal Jacob. Everyone saw a positive change in him. Jacob's personal growth was due in part to the hearts he'd touched over the last few months. Likewise, Uno felt grateful for the privilege of making a positive impact on others' lives. As Uno thought some more, he realized how thankful he was for all the care and support he had received since injuring his leg.

"This is a holy moment," thought Uno. "I think I will use it for the benefit of all."

As Jacob, Tim, and Deb tore into their Christmas gifts, laughing, clapping, and thanking each other, Uno lay his head down next to the warm flames of the fireplace and prayed.

"Oh Mother, Father, God—Infinite and Eternal Power— Universal Conscious Source Energy—Perfect, Loving Presence that is within me and all around me—I shed a tear because I am so grateful today. I am thankful for all the love in my life, all the wisdom, peace, joy, health, beauty, abundance, clarity, and understanding. I am grateful for my loving family and friends, especially my new friends with unique and adaptable abilities, gifts, and qualities. I know for these beautiful souls that they are whole and complete, made in the likeness of their Creator. I know for each that they are perfect as they are, as we all are. I know for each that they release and let go of any thoughts and beliefs related to fear, anger, guilt, shame, lack, limitation, separation, inferiority, disease, or pain—any thoughts that tell them they are anything but perfect creations of a loving and giving Universal Power. I know for anyone who thinks of him or herself as disabled that they see with REAL EYES and REALIZE their spiritual perfection. They are harmony in expression, perfectly balanced in body, mind, and spirit. They love themselves deeply. They accept their bodies and minds as they are, and know they are so much more, being individual expressions of the Infinite and Eternal. I know for each that their spiritual innocence and purity is their birthright, as is their heavy-duty creative power. I know they use this God-given power to create the life they want via their thoughts and beliefs. They are certain of their divinity, and they know who they truly are as spiritual beings. I give thanks again for all the love, for this truth I speak on their behalf, and for my own spiritual and physical perfection as I am healed and loved. I plant these seeds into the inviting spiritual soil of the Universe and know they blossom into complete manifestation. It is done, and so it is."

Here are a few **truth affirmations** and random thoughts related to *living with a "human" disability, appreciating differences, and loving and accepting our "perfect" selves.* They are written in the first-person voice just for you and are "Uno-approved."

- I am whole and complete exactly as I am.
- My body is strong and capable.
- I am grateful for challenges—they always teach me a life lesson.
- I let go of the things I cannot change. I change my mind instead.
- If I fall, I get back up again.
- My strength overpowers my problems.
- The only limitation I have is my thinking, and I can change that.
- The universe has my back—it supports and uplifts me.
- I am an essential part of a greater whole.
- Self-love is the foundation of my wholeness.
- My inner strength tells me that limitations aren't real. My strength is real.
- Persistence and patience guide my thinking.
- I am not my body, I am the confidence, strength, and courage that power me.
- I am divinely led, guided, and inspired in all I think, say, and do.
- I create the life I want by choosing thoughts that strengthen, empower, and guide me.
- I am not fragmented into body parts—I am whole and complete.
- I am a channel for God's strength and power.
- Goodness, strength, and courage govern and master my being.
- Every cell in my body radiates complete harmony and strength.
- I am a being of complete balance and harmony—body, mind, and spirit.
- God is my source, supply, and strength.

- I am blessed beyond my imagination, and I am grateful beyond even that.
- I always expect the best and accept the most.
- I am complete as I am. I let go of any desire to look outside myself for approval.
- I was born complete and am wholly and holy complete in every moment.
- I reject all self-judgment, self-denial, and self-condemnation. I know these are lies posing as the truth, and I accept and embrace my divine perfection.
- The limitations I see are optical delusions. My strength, wholeness, and completeness are God's honest truth.
- My tiny thoughts of sickness, lack, and limitation have no power because they are not true. I know my truth, and it's B.I.G.—Blessed, Inspired, and Grateful.
- I see and know a higher version of myself. My next best Self is always growing and expanding.
- My potential is endless, limitless, and unstoppable.
- The strength that I see in myself is who I become.
- Waves of wholeness and divine perfection wash away all false ideas of limitation and lack.
- I banish all excuses, rationalizations, defenses, and blame from my mind and take complete responsibility for my thoughts, words, and actions.
- While effects, objects, circumstances, and even my body changes, my soul remains whole and complete.
- I choose to be grateful despite any lame and erroneous thoughts of fear and limitation.
- Gratitude anchors me in the present moment, where peace and joy reside.
- I see the upside of all the make-believe downsides.
- I embrace myself and the day ahead with anticipation and a zesty attitude.
- I expect good, I accept good, I embody good, and express good.
- The more thanks I express, the more good I see and experience.

- I count my blessings every day until I lose count and feel at peace.
- I am a work in progress, and I work on myself every day.
- I love and appreciate others by taking care of my thoughts.
- I am a million times stronger than any false thought about weakness or limitation.
- I'm always looking at the bright side of life. I don't even need sunglasses.

Rhyming Affirmations

My body is resilient, capable, flexible, and strong,
Somehow, I've known this all along.

I let go of the things I cannot control,
and know that I'm grateful, happy, complete, and whole.

My strength overpowers every worry and fear,
The path of my progress is totally clear.

A Presence within supports me, it has my back,
It tells me there's no such thing as limitations and lack.

I am not just a body, I am so much more,
Despite my humanness, I am perfect at my core.

God is my strength, my wholeness, and my power,
It helps if I remember this about every half hour.

I create the life I want by choosing my thoughts with care,
I boost my God connection through meditation and prayer.

I expect the best and accept the most.
To limiting thoughts I say, "Adios!"

I see a higher truth, the best version of me,
I am powerful, I am whole, I am loved, I am free.

I'm looking on the bright side, and from here I can see,
That when I seek love within, I create a new me.

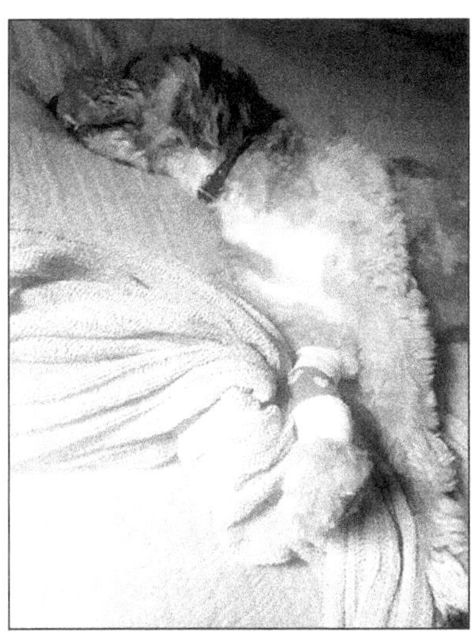

Uno's Random Thoughts

There's a vast difference between being born with a disability and having one thrust upon you. The latter can cause severe emotional challenges. "Should I blindly accept what the doctors are telling me, or should I fight this thing? Maybe I can heal despite what I'm being told. How can I ever have a normal life again? Who will choose to have an intimate relationship with someone like me? My career choices are limited now, and I can never run again, or throw a ball, or be independent." Every story is different, and each person handles their disability in unique ways. The key is to talk about the challenges involved and the resulting feelings. Fear, anger, frustration, guilt, shame, regret, isolation, depression, hopelessness—it all needs to come out and be seen in the light of day. Professional counseling or psychotherapy is essential and very helpful.

Whether someone is diagnosed with a fatal disease, a chronic sickness or condition, or are recovering from a traumatic injury, stroke, or heart attack, they need to stay connected. Engaging in therapy is wise, and beyond that, they need to remain plugged into life. Family, friends, support groups, hobby and interest groups, or social media—staying intertwined with other people. When they're ready, they can go a step further and engage in service to others. Someone once said that helping others is why we are all here, whether we know it or not. Some of us never get out of ourselves; the wise among us lend themselves in service.

Accepting a disability can be harsh, even brutal. Some people don't like to admit defeat. Moving from denial, anger, and fear to acceptance begins the healing process. Here's a quote from the Big Book of Alcoholics Anonymous that has saved many lives. It's relevant to accepting anything that the ego doesn't want to let out of its teeth. "And acceptance is the answer to all my problems today. When I am disturbed, it's because I find some person, place, thing, situation—some fact of my life—unacceptable to me, and I can find no serenity until I accept that person, place, thing, or situation as being exactly the way it is supposed to be at this moment. Nothing, absolutely nothing happens in God's world by mistake. Until I could accept my alcoholism, I could not stay sober. Unless I accept life completely on life's terms, I cannot be happy. I need to concentrate not so much on what needs to be changed in the world as on what needs to be changed in me and in my attitudes."

Being different is good. It's easy and boring to blend in. There are no risks involved in being like everyone else. Being different can be harder, but it's rewarding. There are still people in our society who fear or act critically toward the disabled. They are self-centered, unenlightened, and burdened by false and limiting beliefs. If you're disabled, you just need to ignore these types of people. You also need to disregard the voices (beliefs) in your mind telling you that you're less than. You will become much stronger than the average person. You will learn to connect and be guided by that still, small voice within. The more you turn inward, the louder and more active this God-voice becomes. Some of the strongest, most secure, self-loving, and enlightened people are those who have gone far beyond their disability. Their levels of self-understanding are phenomenal. Because they understand themselves better, they relate to others on a deeper level, and are therefore more kind, empathetic, focused, and useful in service. Being different can lead to an amazing life.

Chapter 12
Life Continues

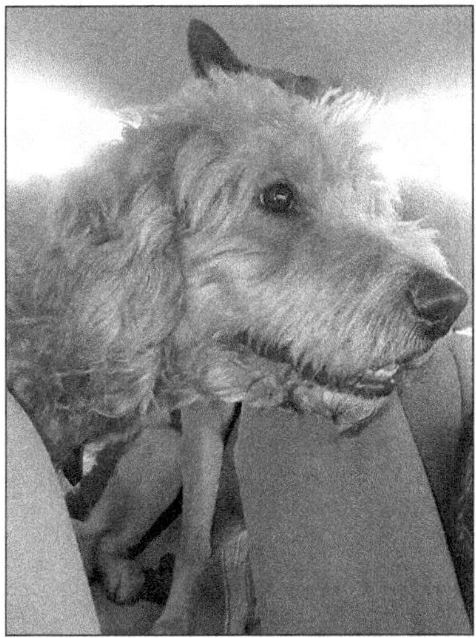

Valentine's Day, 1978—the perfect day for some family love. It was a snow day! Mother Nature dumped eleven inches on Macomb three days prior, so both Deb and Tim took a vacation day and planned a day of sledding. At least one day each year, the two siblings bundled up and headed for their favorite hill behind Thompson Hall on the WIU campus. It was a Tuesday, a school day, so Deb called the high school to tell Mrs. McFadden, the attendance monitor, that Jacob was not feeling well. Deb was the cool foster mom.

Uno and Django could hardly contain their excitement. They knew something was up and could feel the joyous energy exuding from Deb and Tim. When Jacob loaded them into the car, they stumbled and bumbled over each other in the back seat of Tim's cherry red '72 Chevy Chevelle.

"Let's go, let's go!" thought Uno. "I have no idea where we're going, but let's go!"

The college students had broken in the hill over the weekend. The snow was tightly packed. Two wide pathways streamed down the steep 60-foot hill and were almost solid ice from hundreds of previous saucer and sled rides. It was noon and apparently a skip day for the residents of Thompson and her sister dorm, Higgins Hall. About 30 students were already on the hill when Deb, Jacob, Tim, Uno, and Django arrived. Deb and Jacob each carried wide silver saucers, and Tim grunted and gasped for air as he lugged their 20-year-old six-foot wooden toboggan over his head and shoulders. When they reached the crest of the hill and peered down the slope, Deb and Tim looked at each other and grinned like kids. They had been flying down this hill every winter since the 1930s, long before the 19-story twin dormitories loomed over it.

Uno and Django were like caffeine-buzzed flies, running from student to student and back to Deb and Tim. They were in heaven. The college kids loved Uno and Django, especially the girls, who fawned over them like mother hens. A few of the students had saucers and sleds, but most were using cafeteria trays they'd smuggled out of the dorm.

"Let's try out the toboggan first!" shouted Tim.

Deb had to sit in the front of the toboggan, that was the rule. Then Django, then Jacob, then Uno, and Tim anchored the back to ensure weight at the rear. Jacob and Tim hugged their pooches tightly to their bodies. Uno and Django were starry-eyed excited.

"Hey, give us a push!" yelled Tim to a nearby student.

The toboggan inched forward, tilted downward, and dangled over the crest of the hill. As it progressed down the slope, it picked up speed quickly. Then it hit the ice. Whoosh! The world flashed by, the cold wind bit their faces, and the toboggan flew down the hill at a dizzying speed. All Uno could hear was Tim screaming in his ear.

"Wheeeeeeee! Arrrrrrrr! Oh, my gawwwwwwwwd! Ooooooh shit!" Everyone was hollering at the top of their lungs. The toboggan hydroplaned off the ice, bouncing up and down as it screamed down the slope. Blam! It hit the bottom of the hill, sending a kidney punch through their bodies. Still gliding at a fast pace, they continued sailing for another 30 feet, gradually slowing as the toboggan neared the frozen creek.

"Yeah, let's not go ice swimming," thought Deb.

As the toboggan stopped, everyone leaned off, left and right.

"Oh, man, that was great!" screamed Jacob. Uno and Django danced around the toboggan, barking furiously. They loved it!

"Wow, that was fantastic!" thought Uno. "Let's do it again, let's do it again!"

They did, for hours. They tried all combinations—all five on the toboggan—just Deb and Tim—just Jacob, Uno, and Django—Deb, Uno, and Jacob. Tim couldn't remember the last time he laughed so hard. Deb was in heaven, and her face was bright red. Jacob didn't want the day to end.

Then they tried the saucers. They were even faster than the toboggan, zipping down the hill at lightning speed while spinning like a frantic merry-go-round. If you didn't keep a tight grip on the rope handles attached to either side of the saucer, you'd wipe out for sure. They did. Everyone had three or four nasty spills—flying left, hurtling right, diving headfirst—there were splayed bodies tumbling all over that hill while everyone laughed and laughed. Despite all the carnage, there were no concussions, breaks, or sprains, thank God.

It was a miracle if a college student on a cafeteria tray made it all the way down the hill. The trays were precarious. Students were flying down that hill and wiping out on just about every run. If one of the more muscular guys managed to hold onto a tray and survive without crashing, everyone cheered and applauded for him. But that was rare.

After about three hours, everyone was exhausted. The sledding was easy, but all that climbing back up the hill took a toll on Deb's and Tim's aging muscles. Tim was sapped of all energy, lying flat on his back at the top of the hill. Django was on top of him, panting heavily. Deb was sitting on a saucer next to him, Uno on her lap. Jacob continued with his saucer for another half hour. Finally, even the 16-year-old was beginning to fatigue.

"Who's up for some hot chocolate?" shouted Tim.

"Me, me, me!" shouted Deb.

Hot chocolate was another tradition for the siblings. When they were young, they would return home after a long day of sledding, shed their frozen clothes that were stiff as a hardwood board, slip on their jammies, and enjoy a yummy cup of hot chocolate with whipped cream. Their mom, Maxine, had a secret recipe for the best hot chocolate and loved to watch her kids slurp it down while sitting in front of the fireplace, listening to their sledding tales.

These days, they drove two minutes up to the campus' University Union building and sat in Hardee's. The hot chocolate wasn't as good, but it was decent. Deb liked the hot apple pies Hardee's made, and Tim always enjoyed a large order of fries. They sat at a corner table, out of the view of the manager, who frowned upon animals in his classy hamburger joint. Tim treated Uno and Django with two hamburgers each, which they scarfed down within a few seconds. Deb, Tim, and Jacob laughed as they recounted their best and worst saucer runs and wipeouts.

What a day. Uno sat on the floor next to Deb, listening to every word. He thought about how grateful he was for his family, for all the fun they had today, and for his life in general. Uno was having a gratitude moment. A tear ran down each cheek—tears of love and thankfulness.

"I love my life," thought Uno.

That evening, everyone turned in to bed early. Deb was utterly exhausted. Waves of dizzying sleep washed over her as soon as her head hit the pillow. Tim was sore—his knees, ankles, and hips were screaming at him. After taking four aspirin with a cup of warm milk, he was out like a light. Jacob dreamed of flying down a snowy hill, but in his dream, the hill was miles long, and his saucer always faced forward and never overturned.

Uno felt strange as he curled up next to Deb. He was light-headed. His thoughts were few and far between as he slipped into dreamland.

In the wee hours of the morning, Uno awoke. Or was he still dreaming? He wasn't sure. Perhaps he was dreaming that he was awake. As he lay there, he glanced around the bedroom. A dim light appeared in the corner of the room, near the ceiling. As he watched the light, it grew brighter and brighter still.

From the middle of the light, a fog appeared. It drifted down into the room, like a stream of smoke. Uno was transfixed and felt paralyzed, in awe. Something otherworldly was occurring. The fog separated into several separate entities, wisps of semi-distinct shapes. Uno intuitively realized the forms were souls, beings of light. The world was moving in slow motion now as the beings became more distinctive, and clear. They didn't look like bodies, just foggy shapes, but Uno knew they were beings.

They surrounded the bed, floating. At that moment, Uno felt a sense of peace and overwhelming love he had never felt before.

"No, that's not true," thought Uno. "I have felt this kind of love before, many times." It was suddenly so familiar. Uno sensed that he was at home and that the life he had been experiencing as a dog was a dream.

The ghostly figures were now hovering around Uno's head and body, emanating such a powerful essence of love.

Uno thought, "Oh no, I must be dying! No, no, no, I don't want to leave. I want to stay here with Deb and Tim and Jacob. I have more love to give here in this life. I have done so much, and I want to do more."

Images flashed across Uno's mind—Deb, Tim, Jacob, Crystal, Mr. Welker, Chilly, Janiece, the Roe Boat, Chandler Park, the town square—it was like his life was playing on a movie projector. Words and ideas pressed upon his mind. His name, Uno, representing oneness, unity, the One Mind, all of humankind, the oneness of All-That-Is. His life purpose, which he often pondered, was crystal clear now. Miracles! Simple shifts in perceptions, the changing of a mind, a realignment of a thought or belief, powered by unconditional love. His life purpose for the past 20 months seemed so obvious and well defined now.

Uno heard a voice. It was a whisper. He couldn't tell who was speaking or if the sound was male or female. It was not a vocalization, but a whisper in his mind.

"Come home and stay. Stay and come home."

He heard it again. "Come home and stay. Stay and come home."

In that instant, Uno seemed to be drawn from his body, not being pulled, but willingly drawn and attracted to this overpowering feeling of love. At the same time, he felt a strong attachment to his dog body, to Deb, to this world. He was coming, yet staying. Staying yet coming.

The light grew dimmer and dimmer. Blackness. No thought.

Beep, beep, beep! The alarm on Deb's clock radio blared. Deb reached over and shut it off.

Uno awoke. He raised his head and looked around the room.

"Deb, here."

"Love Deb."

"Food, hungry."

"Pee."

"Deb, love Deb."

"Love Tim."

"Love Jacob."

"Love all."

"Love."

"Love."

"Love."

(pause)

"Food."

About the Author

Mark Reed is *born again* every time he is aware of his thoughts. He's a former wild child, recovering alcoholic, student of *A Course in Miracles*, spiritual coach, and loving husband. Mark is a spiritual practitioner licensed by the Centers for Spiritual Living, and author of *The True You: Following your True Self on a Journey of Spiritual Awakening, Lighten Up: New Thought on the Teachings of Jesus*, and *Let's Get Metaphysical: De-Coding the Teachings of Jesus*. He has taught many classes on metaphysical Bible interpretation, affirmative prayer, oneness, mental discipline, ego relinquishment, visioning, and meditation. A dedicated student of New Thought philosophy and the Science of Mind, he's an inspiring Facebook presence, and has written a myriad of spiritual self-help articles for publication. His interests are helping others know their own spiritual truth via spiritual coaching, creating insightful and humorous memes for his Facebook pages, and writing about himself in the third person. Mark's spiritual home is the West Valley Center for Spiritual Living in Peoria, AZ and he and his beautiful wife Dora reside in nearby Avondale. Contact Mark via his Facebook page, "Mark Reed, New Thought Author" and purchase his other works at AuthorMarkReed.com.

Other Books by Mark Reed

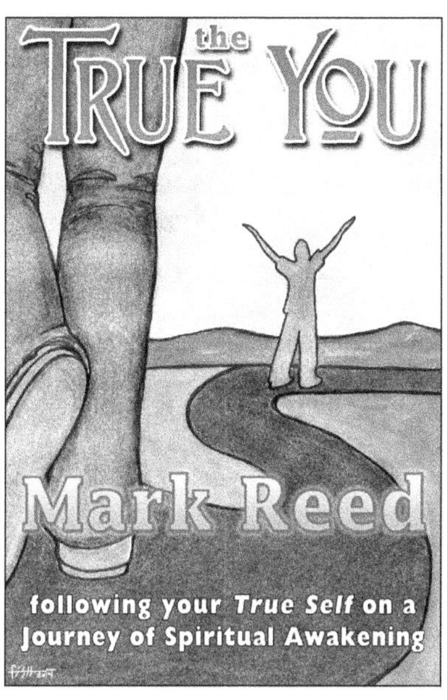

Available on Amazon.com

www.ingramcontent.com/pod-product-compliance
Lightning Source LLC
Chambersburg PA
CBHW071438130726
47997CB00006B/2139